SBAC

Math Workbook

for

Grade 4

Abundant Exercises and Two

Full-Length SBAC Math

Practice Tests

Michael Smith & Reza Nazari

SBAC Math Workbook for Grade 4

Published in the United State of America By

The Math Notion

Email: info@Mathnotion.com

Web: www.MathNotion.com

SBAC MATH WORKBOOK FOR GRADE 4

SBAC Math Workbooks covers all Math topics you will ever need to prepare for the SBAC Math test. This workbook contains the key areas of the SBAC Math. It reviews the most important components of the SBAC test. This workbook offers plenty of practice questions to challenge students for achieving the high score on their real SBAC Math test. SBAC Math Workbook is the ideal prep solution for anyone who wants to pass the SBAC Math test. Not only does it provide abundant math exercises, but it also contains practice test questions as well as detailed explanations of each answer.

This Math workbook is filled with exercises and worksheets covering fundamental math, arithmetic, algebra, geometry, basic statistics, probability, and data analysis. Answers are provided for all math questions, and two full-length SBAC Math tests with detailed answers and explanations can help you discover your weak areas for concentrated study. Here is comprehensive preparation for the SBAC Math section, and a valuable learning tool for the SBAC test takers who need to improve their knowledge of Mathematics and prepare for the SBAC Math test.

Each chapter and topic of the book go into detail to cover all the content likely to appear on the SBAC test. This completely revised edition reflects all the new types of math questions that will appear on the SBAC.

Developed by experienced SBAC Math teachers and authors for test takers trying to achieve a passing score on the SBAC test, this comprehensive Math workbook includes:

- Over 2,000 revised Math questions to practice with

- Easy–to–follow activities

- Fun and interactive exercises that build confidence

- Topics are grouped by category, so you can easily focus on the topics you struggle on

- 2 Full-length and REAL SBAC Math tests

- Detailed answers and explanations for the SBAC Math practice tests

After completing this workbook, you will gain confidence, strong foundation, and adequate practice to ace the SBAC Math test.

Get the help and confidence you need to be well prepared for the SBAC Math test!

About the Author

Michael Smith has been a math instructor for over a decade now. He holds a master's degree in Management. Since 2006, Michael has devoted his time to both teaching and developing exceptional math learning materials. As a Math instructor and test prep expert, Michael has worked with thousands of students. He has used the feedback of his students to develop a unique study program that can be used by students to drastically improve their math score fast and effectively.

– Common Core Math Workbook

– PARRC Math Workbook

– PSSA Math Workbook

– FSA Math Workbook

– GED Math Workbook

– HiSET Math Workbook

– and many Math Education Workbooks...

As an experienced Math teacher, Mr. Smith employs a variety of formats to help students achieve their goals: He tutors online and in person, he teaches students in large groups, and he provides training materials and textbooks through his website and through Amazon.

You can contact Michael via email at:

info@Mathnotion.com

WWW.MathNotion.COM

... So Much More Online!

✓ FREE Math lessons

✓ More Math learning books!

✓ Mathematics Worksheets

✓ Online Math Tutors

Need a PDF version of this book?

Please visit www.MathNotion.com

Contents

Chapter 1: Place Vales and Number Sense

Topics that you'll learn in this chapter:

- ✓ Place Values
- ✓ Compare Numbers
- ✓ Numbers in Word
- ✓ Roman Numerals
- ✓ Rounding
- ✓ Odd or Even
- ✓ Pattern
- ✓ Growing Pattern

Place Values

✎ Write numbers in expanded form.

1) Thirty–five   ___ + ___

2) forty–seven   ___ + ___

3) sixty–two   ___ + ___

4) fifty–nine   ___ + ___

5) Ninety–two   ___ + ___

✎ Circle the correct choice.

6) The 3 in 83 is in the

       Ones place   tens place   hundreds place

7) The 5 in 59 is in the

       Ones place   tens place   hundreds place

8) The 4 in 824 is in the

       Ones place   tens place   hundreds place

9) The 9 in 690 is in the

       Ones place   tens place   hundreds place

10) The 7 in 751 is in the

       Ones place   tens place   hundreds place

Comparing and Ordering Numbers

✎ *Use less than, equal to or greater than.*

1) 32 _____ 36

2) 86 _____ 99

3) 49 _____ 25

4) 36 _____ 32

5) 85 _____ 85

6) 59 _____ 52

7) 89 _____ 79

8) 58 _____ 45

9) 66 _____ 66

10) 86 _____ 98

11) 36 _____ 46

12) 69 _____ 58

13) 78 _____ 69

14) 12 _____ 34

✎ *Order each set numbers from least to greatest.*

15) − 13, − 18, 20, − 3, 1   ___, ___, ___, ___, ___, ___

16) 8, − 6, 5, − 4, 2   ___, ___, ___, ___, ___, ___

17) 16, − 44, 20, 0, − 22   ___, ___, ___, ___, ___, ___

18) 26, − 96, 0, − 13, 67, − 55 ___, ___, ___, ___, ___, ___

19) − 17, − 71, 90, − 25, − 59, − 39 ___, ___, ___, ___, ___, ___

20) 98, 5, 46, 19, 88, 24   ___, ___, ___, ___, ___, ___

Write Numbers in Words

✍ Write each number in words.

1) 534 _____

2) 802 _____

3) 630 _____

4) 372 _____

5) 265 _____

6) 901 _____

7) 1,218 _____

8) 1,364 _____

9) 3,373 _____

10) 2,485 _____

11) 7,672 _____

12) 6,490 _____

13) 3,146 _____

14) 5,012 _____

Roman Numerals

1	I	11	XI	21	XXI
2	II	12	XII	22	XXII
3	III	13	XIII	23	XXIII
4	IV	14	XIV	24	XXIV
5	V	15	XV	25	XXV
6	VI	16	XVI	26	XXVI
7	VII	17	XVII	27	XXVII
8	VIII	18	XVIII	28	XXVIII
9	IX	19	XIX	29	XXIX
10	X	20	XX	30	XXX

✍ *Write in Romans numerals.*

1) 1 _____   2) 6 _____

3) 3 _____   4) 9 _____

5) 15 _____   6) 8 _____

7) 4 _____   8) 2 _____

9) 7 _____   10) 5 _____

11) Add 8 + 2 and write in Roman numerals.   _____

12) Add 6 + 5 and write in Roman numerals.   _____

13) Subtract 12 – 10 and write in Roman numerals. _____

Rounding Numbers

Round each number to the underlined place value.

1) 1982

2) 3,995

3) 5364

4) 1281

5) 2355

6) 1334

7) 1,203

8) 1457

9) 7483

10) 1913

11) 4539

12) 9,125

13) 8,452

14) 2579

15) 1,230

16) 7698

17) 9493

18) 5239

19) 2491

20) 2,924

21) 9,945

22) 5555

23) 6939

24) 9869

Odd or Even

Identify whether each number is even or odd.

1) 14 _____   7) 32 _____

2) 3 _____   8) 17 _____

3) 23 _____   9) 64 _____

4) 16 _____   10) 36 _____

5) 33 _____   11) 13 _____

6) 77 _____   12) 79 _____

Circle the even number in each group.

13) 22, 11, 57, 13, 19, 47   15) 19, 35, 24, 57, 65, 49

14) 15, 17, 27, 23, 33, 26   16) 67, 58, 89, 63, 27, 63

Circle the odd number in each group.

17) 12, 14, 22, 64, 53, 98   19) 46, 82, 63, 98, 64, 56

18) 16, 26, 28, 44, 62, 73   20) 27, 92, 58, 36, 38, 72

Repeating Pattern

Circle the picture that comes next in each picture pattern.

1)

2)

3)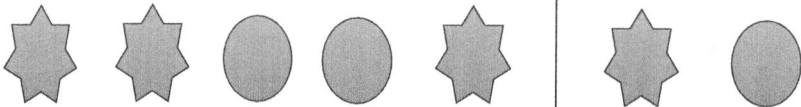

4)

5)

Growing Patterns

✍ *Draw the picture that comes next in each growing pattern.*

1)

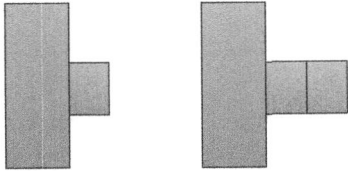

2)

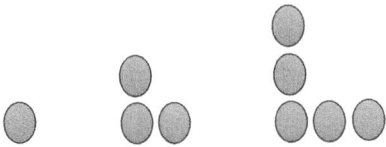

3)

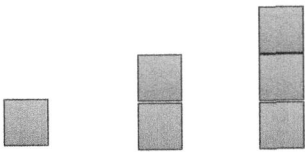

4)

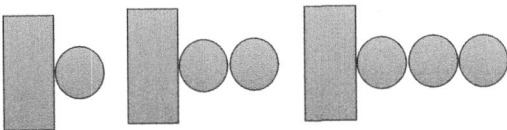

5)

Patterns: Numbers

✍ *Write the numbers that come next.*

1) 4, 8, 12, 16,   ____, ____, ____, ____

2) 7, 14, 21, 28,   ____, ____, ____, ____

3) 10, 20, 30, 40,   ____, ____, ____, ____

4) 13, 23, 33, 43,   ____, ____, ____, ____

5) 7, 12, 17, 22,   ____, ____, ____, ____

6) 10, 14, 18, 22, 26,   ____, ____, ____, ____

✍ *Write the next three numbers in each counting sequence.*

1) −31, −22, −13, _____, _____, _____, _____

2) 453, 441, 429, _____, _____, _____, _____

3) 13, 23, _____, _____, 53, _____

4) 21, 30, _____, _____, _____

5) 55, 45, _____, _____, _____

6) 62, 51, 40, _____, _____, _____

7) 64, 55, 46, _____, _____, _____

8) What are the next three numbers in this counting sequence? 1450, 1650, 1850, _____, _____, _____

9) What is the seventh number in this counting sequence?

5, 12, 19, _____

Answers of Worksheets – Chapter 1

Place Values

1) 30 + 5

2) 40 + 7

3) 60 + 2

4) 50 + 9

5) 90 + 2

6) ones place

7) tens place

8) ones place

9) tens place

10) hundreds place

Comparing and Ordering Numbers

1) 32 less than 36

2) 86 less than 99

3) 49 greater than 25

4) 36 greater than 32

5) 85 equals to 85

6) 59 greater than 52

7) 89 greater than 79

8) 58 greater than 45

9) 66 equals to 66

10) 86 less than 98

11) 36 less than 46

12) 69 greater than 58

13) 78 greater than 69

14) 12 less than 34

15) −18, −13, −3, 1, 20

16) −6, −4, 2, 5, 8

17) −44, −22, 0, 16, 20

18) −96, −55, −13, 0, 26, 67

19) −71, −59, −39, −25, −17, 90

20) 5, 19, 24, 46, 88, 98

Word Names for Numbers

1) five hundred thirty-four

2) eight hundred two

3) six hundred thirty

4) three hundred seventy-two

5) two hundred sixty-five

6) nine hundred one

7) one thousand, two hundred eighteen

8) one thousand, three hundred sixty-four

9) three thousand, three hundred seventy-three

10) two thousand, four hundred eighty-five

11) seven thousand, six hundred seventy-two

12) six thousand, four hundred ninety

13) three thousand, one hundred forty-six

14) five thousand, twelve

Roman Numerals

1) I	6) VIII	11) X
2) VI	7) IV	12) XI
3) III	8) II	13) II
4) IX	9) VII	
5) XV	10) V	

Rounding Numbers

1) 2000	9) 7500	17) 9490
2) 4000	10) 1910	18) 5240
3) 5360	11) 4540	19) 2490
4) 1280	12) 9000	20) 2900
5) 2360	13) 8450	21) 10,000
6) 1330	14) 2600	22) 5560
7) 1200	15) 1200	23) 6900
8) 1460	16) 7700	24) 9870

Odd or Even

1) even	5) odd	9) even
2) odd	6) odd	10) even
3) odd	7) even	11) even
4) even	8) odd	12) odd

13) 22

14) 26

15) 24

16) 58

17) 53

18) 73

19) 63

20) 27

Repeating pattern

1)

2)

3)

4)

5)

Growing patterns

1)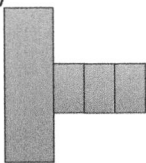

2)

3)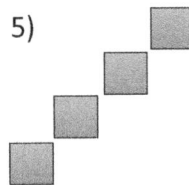

4)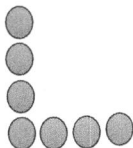

5)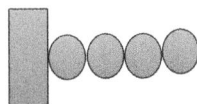

Patterns: Numbers

1) 4, 8, 12, 16, 20, 24, 28, 32

2) 7, 14, 21, 28, 35, 42, 49, 56

3) 10, 20, 30, 40, 50, 60, 70, 80

4) 13, 23, 33, 43,   53, 63, 73, 83

5) 7, 12, 17, 22,   27, 32, 37, 42

6) 10, 14, 18, 22, 26, 30, 34, 38

Patterns

1) −4, 5, 14, 23

2) 417, 405, 393

3) 13−23−33−43−53−63

4) 39−48−57

5) 35−25−15

6) 29,18,7

7) 37,28, 19

8) 2050−2250−2450

9) 47

Chapter 2: Whole Number Operations

Topics that you'll learn in this chapter:

❖ **Adding and Subtracting:**

✓ Adding Three–Digit Numbers

✓ Adding Hundreds

✓ Adding 4–Digit Numbers

✓ Subtracting 4–Digit Numbers

❖ **Multiplication and Division**

✓ Multiplication

✓ Division

✓ Long Division by One Digit

✓ Division with Remainders

Adding Three–Digit Numbers

✎Find each sum.

1)
$$794 + 216$$

4)
$$560 + 480$$

7)
$$786 + 256$$

2)
$$462 + 139$$

5)
$$837 + 360$$

8)
$$916 + 417$$

3)
$$145 + 167$$

6)
$$335 + 109$$

9)
$$996 + 108$$

Find the missing numbers.

10) $419 + \underline{\quad} = 770$

11) $500 + 400 = \underline{\quad}$

12) $372 + \underline{\quad} = 524$

13) $860 + \underline{\quad} = 925$

14) $\underline{\quad} + 537 = 804$

15) $\underline{\quad} + 720 = 915$

16) Leon sells phones. He buys a phone for $675. Then, he purchases a different brand for the bargain price of $518. How much does Leon spend on the two phones?

Subtracting 3–Digit Numbers

✏ *Subtract.*

1) $619 - 425$

2) $500 - 274$

3) $1{,}051 - 875$

4) $760 - 714$

5) $810 - 605$

6) $618 - 205$

7) $426 - 339$

8) $200 - 121$

9) $186 - 98$

✏ *Find the missing number.*

10) $625 - \_\_ = 208$

11) $872 - \_\_ = 320$

12) $920 - 576 = \_\_$

13) $567 - \_\_ = 107$

14) $398 - 189 = \_\_$

15) $424 - 364 = \_\_$

16) Amity has $700 in the checking account. She paid $462 for rent. How much money does she have in her account now?

Adding and subtracting Hundreds

Add.

1) 300 + 200 = - - -

2) 400 + 200 = - - -

3) 900 + 200 = - - -

4) 700 + 100 = - - -

5) 100 + 600 = - - -

6) 400 + 600 = - - -

7) 500 + 800 = - - -

8) 400 + 100 = - - -

9) 400 + 500 = - - -

10) 300 + 400 = - - -

11) 300 + 300 = - - -

12) 500 + 200 = - - -

Subtract.

1) 700 − 200 = - - -

2) 900 − 300 = - - -

3) 1000 − 600 = - - -

4) 800 − 100 = - - -

5) 600 − 300 = - - -

6) 900 − 200 = - - -

7) 800 − 700 = - - -

8) 200 − 200 = - - -

9) 400 − 200 = - - -

10) 300 − 100 = - - -

11) 700 − 500 = - - -

12) 500 − 200 =- - -

Adding 4–Digit Numbers

✎ *Add.*

21)
$$\begin{array}{r} 1,250 \\ + 4,687 \\ \hline \end{array}$$

24)
$$\begin{array}{r} 3,837 \\ +2,595 \\ \hline \end{array}$$

27)
$$\begin{array}{r} 8,158 \\ + 1,263 \\ \hline \end{array}$$

22)
$$\begin{array}{r} 6,158 \\ + 2,269 \\ \hline \end{array}$$

25)
$$\begin{array}{r} 7,230 \\ +4,098 \\ \hline \end{array}$$

28)
$$\begin{array}{r} 6,006 \\ + 3,994 \\ \hline \end{array}$$

23)
$$\begin{array}{r} 3,754 \\ + 2,462 \\ \hline \end{array}$$

26)
$$\begin{array}{r} 5,906 \\ +2,099 \\ \hline \end{array}$$

29)
$$\begin{array}{r} 9,417 \\ +1,374 \\ \hline \end{array}$$

✎ *Find the missing numbers.*

30) $1,107 + \underline{\quad} = 4,376$

31) $1,650 + 1,400 = \underline{\quad}$

32) $4,267 + \underline{\quad} = 6,200$

33) $1,750 + \underline{\quad} = 3,405$

34) $\underline{\quad} + 5,630 = 8,250$

35) $\underline{\quad} + 7,860 = 9,257$

36) David sells gems. He finds a diamond in Istanbul and buys it for $4,750. Then, he flies to Cairo and purchases a bigger diamond for the bargain price of $3,905. How much does David spend on the two diamonds?

Subtracting 4–Digit Numbers

✎ *Subtract.*

1)
$$\begin{array}{r} 7,519 \\ -\ 5,462 \\ \hline \end{array}$$

4)
$$\begin{array}{r} 8,756 \\ -\ 6,762 \\ \hline \end{array}$$

7)
$$\begin{array}{r} 5,158 \\ -\ 1,268 \\ \hline \end{array}$$

2)
$$\begin{array}{r} 6,262 \\ -\ 4,375 \\ \hline \end{array}$$

5)
$$\begin{array}{r} 9,290 \\ -\ 3,829 \\ \hline \end{array}$$

8)
$$\begin{array}{r} 4,700 \\ -\ 2,612 \\ \hline \end{array}$$

3)
$$\begin{array}{r} 7,821 \\ -\ 3,212 \\ \hline \end{array}$$

6)
$$\begin{array}{r} 6,110 \\ -5,216 \\ \hline \end{array}$$

9)
$$\begin{array}{r} 3,230 \\ -1,542 \\ \hline \end{array}$$

✎ *Find the missing number.*

10) $2320 - \underline{\hspace{1cm}} = 1125$

13) $2550 - \underline{\hspace{1cm}} = 1245$

11) $6574 - \underline{\hspace{1cm}} = 5605$

14) $8780 - 7890 = \underline{\hspace{1cm}}$

12) $3124 - 1578 = \underline{\hspace{1cm}}$

15) $4080 - 2560 = \underline{\hspace{1cm}}$

16) Jackson had $3,560 invested in the stock market until he lost $1,702 on those investments. How much money does he have in the stock market now?

Multiplication

✎ *Find the answers.*

1)
$$\begin{array}{r} 42 \\ \times\ 13 \\ \hline \\ \hline \end{array}$$

4)
$$\begin{array}{r} 530 \\ \times\ 4 \\ \hline \\ \hline \end{array}$$

7)
$$\begin{array}{r} 470 \\ \times\ 34 \\ \hline \\ \hline \end{array}$$

2)
$$\begin{array}{r} 35 \\ \times\ 10 \\ \hline \\ \hline \end{array}$$

5)
$$\begin{array}{r} 265 \\ \times\ 5 \\ \hline \\ \hline \end{array}$$

8)
$$\begin{array}{r} 952 \\ \times\ 26 \\ \hline \\ \hline \end{array}$$

3)
$$\begin{array}{r} 120 \\ \times\ 8 \\ \hline \\ \hline \end{array}$$

6)
$$\begin{array}{r} 89 \\ \times\ 35 \\ \hline \\ \hline \end{array}$$

9)
$$\begin{array}{r} 391 \\ \times\ 63 \\ \hline \\ \hline \end{array}$$

10) The Haunted House Ride runs 4 times a day. It has 5 cars, each of which can hold 7 people. How many people can ride the Haunted House Ride in one day?

11) Each train car has 2 rows of seats. There are 6 seats in each row. How many seats are there in 5 train cars?

Division

✎ *Find each missing number.*

1) $15 \div \underline{\quad} = 1$

2) $48 \div 4 = \underline{\quad}$

3) $88 \div \underline{\quad} = 8$

4) $50 \div 10 = \underline{\quad}$

5) $33 \div \underline{\quad} = 3$

6) $16 \div \underline{\quad} = 8$

7) $\underline{\quad} \div 10 = 6$

8) $120 \div 12 = \underline{\quad}$

9) $16 \div \underline{\quad} = 1$

10) $80 \div \underline{\quad} = 8$

11) $\underline{\quad} \div 11 = 5$

12) $\underline{\quad} \div 12 = 12$

13) $60 \div \underline{\quad} = 6$

14) $\underline{\quad} \div 11 = 13$

15) $48 \div 12 = \underline{\quad}$

16) $30 \div 10 = \underline{\quad}$

17) $11 \div 11 = \underline{\quad}$

18) $132 \div \underline{\quad} = 12$

19) Anna has 140 books. She wants to put them in equal numbers on 14 bookshelves. How many books can she put on a bookshelf? _____ books

20) If dividend is 88 and the quotient is 11, then what is the divisor? ___

Long Division by One Digit

✏️ *Find the quotient.*

1) $5\overline{)660}$

2) $7\overline{)525}$

3) $3\overline{)387}$

4) $9\overline{)117}$

5) $4\overline{)136}$

6) $6\overline{)126}$

7) $8\overline{)184}$

8) $2\overline{)534}$

9) $5\overline{)185}$

10) $4\overline{)144}$

11) $3\overline{)267}$

12) $9\overline{)432}$

13) $7\overline{)1008}$

14) $5\overline{)640}$

15) $8\overline{)1136}$

16) $9\overline{)3114}$

17) $6\overline{)1224}$

18) $3\overline{)2559}$

Division with Remainders

✏️ *Find the quotient with remainder.*

1) $8\overline{)948}$

2) $6\overline{)589}$

3) $2\overline{)185}$

4) $9\overline{)382}$

5) $3\overline{)440}$

6) $7\overline{)673}$

7) $6\overline{)595}$

8) $3\overline{)394}$

9) $7\overline{)1130}$

10) $4\overline{)558}$

11) $6\overline{)1864}$

12) $9\overline{)3958}$

13) $8\overline{)1085}$

14) $5\overline{)5277}$

Answers of Worksheets – Chapter 2

Adding three–digit numbers

1) 1,010	5) 1,197	9) 1,104	13) 65
2) 601	6) 444	10) 351	14) 267
3) 312	7) 1,042	11) 900	15) 195
4) 1,040	8) 1,333	12) 152	16) 1,193

Subtracting three–digit numbers

1) 194	5) 205	9) 88	13) 460
2) 226	6) 413	10) 417	14) 209
3) 176	7) 87	11) 552	15) 60
4) 46	8) 79	12) 344	16) 238

Adding hundreds

1) 500	4) 800	7) 1,300	10) 700
2) 600	5) 700	8) 500	11) 600
3) 1,100	6) 1,000	9) 900	12) 700

subtracting hundreds

1) 500	4) 700	7) 100	10) 200
2) 600	5) 300	8) 0	11) 200
3) 400	6) 700	9) 200	12) 300

Adding 4–digit numbers

1) 5,937	5) 11,328	9) 10,791	13) 1,655
2) 8,427	6) 8,005	10) 3,269	14) 2,620
3) 6,216	7) 9,421	11) 3,050	15) 1397
4) 6,432	8) 10,000	12) 1,933	16) $8,655

Subtracting 4–digit numbers

1) 2,057	2) 1,887	3) 4,609	4) 1,994

5) 5,461	8) 2,088	11) 969	14) 890
6) 894	9) 1,688	12) 1,546	15) 1520
7) 3,890	10) 1,195	13) 1,305	16) 1,858

Multiplication

1) 546	4) 2,120	7) 15,980	10) 140
2) 350	5) 1,325	8) 24,752	11) 60
3) 960	6) 3,115	9) 24,633	

Division

1) 15	6) 2	11) 55	16) 3
2) 12	7) 60	12) 144	17) 1
3) 11	8) 10	13) 10	18) 11
4) 5	9) 16	14) 143	19) 10
5) 11	10) 10	15) 4	20) 8

Long Division by One Digit

1) 132	6) 21	11) 89	16) 346
2) 75	7) 23	12) 48	17) 204
3) 129	8) 267	13) 144	18) 853
4) 13	9) 37	14) 128	
5) 34	10) 36	15) 142	

Division with Remainders

1) 118 R4	6) 96 R1	11) 310 R4
2) 98 R1	7) 99 R1	12) 439 R7
3) 92 R1	8) 131 R1	13) 135 R5
4) 42 R4	9) 161 R3	14) 1,055 R2
5) 146 R2	10) 139 R2	

Chapter 3: Mixed operations

Topics that you'll learn in this chapter:

- ✓ Rounding and Estimating
- ✓ Estimate Sums
- ✓ Estimate Differences
- ✓ Estimate Products
- ✓ Missing Numbers

Rounding and Estimating

Round each number to the underlined place value.

1) 9̲63

2) 4,9̲97

3) 6̲4

4) 8̲3

5) 5̲7

6) 73̲2

7) 2,2̲06

8) 9.5̲8

9) 8.4̲84

10) 12̲.3170

Estimate the sum by rounding each added to the nearest ten.

11) 65 + 9

12) 14 + 73

13) 63 + 7

14) 33 + 27

15) 14 + 96

16) 32 + 12

17) 49 + 87

18) 35 + 4

19) 56 + 73

20) 53 + 59

21) 13 + 67

22) 72 + 32

23) 42 + 66

24) 55 + 65

25) 563 + 231

26) 724 + 176

Estimate Sums

✍ *Estimate the sum by rounding each added to the nearest*

ten.

1) 66 + 9

2) 14 + 83

3) 77 + 7

4) 23 + 37

5) 15 + 63

6) 26 + 11

7) 49 + 77

8) 45 + 4

9) 51 + 73

10) 34 + 59

11) 14 + 46

12) 52 + 12

13) 42 + 55

14) 32 + 75

15) 553 + 243

16) 52 + 77

17) 86 + 84

18) 39 + 89

19) 68 + 74

20) 39 + 27

21) 91 + 68

22) 56 + 81

23) 24 + 96

24) 42 + 69

Estimate Differences

Estimate the difference by rounding each number to the nearest ten.

1) 46 – 10

2) 23 – 12

3) 65 – 36

4) 33 – 13

5) 68 – 36

6) 32 – 11

7) 67 – 37

8) 36 – 19

9) 84 – 35

10) 68 – 43

11) 56 – 16

12) 75 – 27

13) 53 – 33

14) 75 – 32

15) 92 – 63

16) 45 – 32

17) 89 – 74

18) 43 – 11

19) 47 – 39

20) 98 – 36

21) 93 – 78

22) 77 – 23

23) 99 – 14

24) 86 – 43

Estimate Products

✎ *Estimate the products.*

1) 25×18

2) 15×17

3) 32×25

4) 52×12

5) 67×22

6) 37×92

7) 52×92

8) 19×38

9) 23×14

10) 84×42

11) 52×32

12) 69×12

13) 36×22

14) 73×59

15) 53×88

16) 37×72

17) 37×92

18) 42×28

19) 43×37

20) 54×93

21) 88×72

22) 66×22

23) 54×13

24) 98×63

Missing Numbers

Find the missing numbers.

1) $20 \times \underline{} = 80$

2) $16 \times \underline{} = 48$

3) $\underline{} \times 14 = 70$

4) $16 \times \underline{} = 96$

5) $\underline{} \times 19 = 133$

6) $17 \times \underline{} = 51$

7) $\underline{} \times 1 = 15$

8) $22 \times \underline{} = 66$

9) $30 \times \underline{} = 120$

10) $12 \times 7 = \underline{}$

11) $18 \times 5 = \underline{}$

12) $22 \times 4 = \underline{}$

13) $23 \times 3 = \underline{}$

14) $\underline{} \times 25 = 125$

15) $24 \times \underline{} = 144$

16) $20 \times 4 = \underline{}$

17) $20 \times \underline{} = 160$

18) $15 \times \underline{} = 135$

19) $\underline{} \times 15 = 90$

20) $21 \times 4 = \underline{}$

21) $\underline{} \times 20 = 160$

22) $19 \times \underline{} = 95$

23) $22 \times 5 = \underline{}$

24) $25 \times 9 = \underline{}$

25) $\underline{} \times 18 = 126$

26) $42 \times \underline{} = 84$

Answers of Worksheets – Chapter 3

Rounding and Estimating

1) 1,000	10) 12	19) 130
2) 5,000	11) 80	20) 110
3) 660	12) 80	21) 80
4) 80	13) 70	22) 100
5) 60	14) 60	23) 110
6) 730	15) 110	24) 130
7) 2,200	16) 40	25) 790
8) 9.6	17) 140	26) 900
9) 8.5	18) 40	

Estimate sums

1) 80	9) 120	17) 170
2) 90	10) 90	18) 130
3) 90	11) 60	19) 140
4) 60	12) 60	20) 70
5) 80	13) 100	21) 160
6) 40	14) 110	22) 130
7) 130	15) 790	23) 120
8) 50	16) 130	24) 110

Estimate differences

1) 40	6) 20	11) 40
2) 10	7) 30	12) 50
3) 30	8) 20	13) 20
4) 20	9) 50	14) 50
5) 30	10) 30	15) 30

16) 20

17) 20

18) 30

19) 10

20) 60

21) 10

22) 60

23) 90

24) 50

Estimate products

1) 600

2) 400

3) 900

4) 500

5) 1400

6) 3600

7) 4500

8) 800

9) 200

10) 3200

11) 1500

12) 700

13) 800

14) 4200

15) 4500

16) 2800

17) 3600

18) 1200

19) 1600

20) 4500

21) 6300

22) 1400

23) 500

24) 6000

Missing Numbers

1) 4

2) 3

3) 5

4) 6

5) 7

6) 3

7) 15

8) 3

9) 4

10) 84

11) 90

12) 88

13) 69

14) 5

15) 6

16) 80

17) 8

18) 9

19) 6

20) 84

21) 8

22) 5

23) 110

24) 225

25) 7

26) 2

Chapter 4: Fractions and Mixed Numbers

Topics that you'll learn in this chapter:

- ✓ Simplifying Fractions
- ✓ Add and Subtract Fractions with Like Denominators
- ✓ Compare Fractions with Like Denominators
- ✓ More than two Fractions with Like Denominators
- ✓ Add and Subtract Fractions with Unlike Denominators
- ✓ Ordering Fractions
- ✓ Add and Subtract Fractions with Denominators of 10, 100, and 1000
- ✓ Fractions to Mixed Numbers
- ✓ Mixed Numbers to Fractions
- ✓ Add and Subtract Mixed Numbers with Like Denominators

Simplifying Fractions

✐Simplify the fractions.

1) $\dfrac{44}{84}$

2) $\dfrac{6}{15}$

3) $\dfrac{12}{16}$

4) $\dfrac{6}{36}$

5) $\dfrac{12}{24}$

6) $\dfrac{5}{35}$

7) $\dfrac{14}{49}$

8) $\dfrac{12}{36}$

9) $\dfrac{40}{50}$

10) $\dfrac{6}{42}$

11) $\dfrac{27}{81}$

12) $\dfrac{21}{14}$

13) $\dfrac{35}{49}$

14) $\dfrac{48}{64}$

15) $\dfrac{15}{75}$

16) $\dfrac{55}{88}$

17) $\dfrac{21}{56}$

18) $\dfrac{15}{40}$

19) $\dfrac{9}{81}$

20) $\dfrac{60}{80}$

Like Denominators

✎*Add fractions.*

1) $\dfrac{3}{4} + \dfrac{1}{4}$

2) $\dfrac{3}{7} + \dfrac{4}{7}$

3) $\dfrac{7}{8} + \dfrac{4}{8}$

4) $\dfrac{3}{5} + \dfrac{3}{5}$

5) $\dfrac{4}{12} + \dfrac{3}{12}$

6) $\dfrac{3}{8} + \dfrac{2}{8}$

7) $\dfrac{4}{7} + \dfrac{4}{7}$

8) $\dfrac{5}{13} + \dfrac{7}{13}$

9) $\dfrac{5}{18} + \dfrac{12}{18}$

10) $\dfrac{8}{12} + \dfrac{5}{12}$

11) $\dfrac{5}{16} + \dfrac{5}{16}$

12) $\dfrac{5}{25} + \dfrac{12}{25}$

13) $\dfrac{8}{17} + \dfrac{9}{17}$

14) $\dfrac{7}{20} + \dfrac{5}{20}$

15) $\dfrac{9}{13} + \dfrac{3}{13}$

16) $\dfrac{18}{35} + \dfrac{15}{35}$

17) $\dfrac{12}{27} + \dfrac{11}{27}$

18) $\dfrac{4}{15} + \dfrac{9}{15}$

19) $\dfrac{22}{42} + \dfrac{11}{42}$

20) $\dfrac{8}{33} + \dfrac{15}{33}$

21) $\dfrac{15}{30} + \dfrac{12}{30}$

22) $\dfrac{1}{7} + \dfrac{6}{7}$

23) $\dfrac{3}{8} + \dfrac{2}{8}$

24) $\dfrac{5}{9} + \dfrac{2}{9}$

25) $\dfrac{3}{10} + \dfrac{4}{10}$

26) $\dfrac{7}{10} + \dfrac{1}{10}$

27) $\dfrac{4}{7} + \dfrac{2}{7}$

28) $\dfrac{4}{6} + \dfrac{2}{6}$

29) $\dfrac{1}{11} + \dfrac{1}{11}$

30) $\dfrac{12}{25} + \dfrac{5}{25}$

✍ Subtract fractions.

1) $\dfrac{6}{7} - \dfrac{2}{7}$

2) $\dfrac{4}{5} - \dfrac{1}{5}$

3) $\dfrac{5}{11} - \dfrac{4}{11}$

4) $\dfrac{7}{8} - \dfrac{2}{8}$

5) $\dfrac{7}{10} - \dfrac{3}{10}$

6) $\dfrac{8}{7} - \dfrac{3}{7}$

7) $\dfrac{7}{9} - \dfrac{5}{9}$

8) $\dfrac{10}{15} - \dfrac{9}{15}$

9) $\dfrac{8}{13} - \dfrac{5}{13}$

10) $\dfrac{9}{12} - \dfrac{8}{12}$

11) $\dfrac{18}{24} - \dfrac{12}{24}$

12) $\dfrac{10}{21} - \dfrac{8}{21}$

13) $\dfrac{12}{27} - \dfrac{11}{27}$

14) $\dfrac{25}{36} - \dfrac{17}{36}$

15) $\dfrac{21}{27} - \dfrac{10}{27}$

16) $\dfrac{27}{45} - \dfrac{15}{45}$

17) $\dfrac{31}{37} - \dfrac{26}{37}$

18) $\dfrac{18}{26} - \dfrac{8}{26}$

19) $\dfrac{35}{45} - \dfrac{15}{45}$

20) $\dfrac{29}{30} - \dfrac{19}{30}$

21) $\dfrac{22}{38} - \dfrac{11}{38}$

22) $\dfrac{3}{5} - \dfrac{2}{5}$

23) $\dfrac{5}{7} - \dfrac{3}{7}$

24) $\dfrac{3}{4} - \dfrac{2}{4}$

25) $\dfrac{8}{10} - \dfrac{3}{10}$

26) $\dfrac{6}{12} - \dfrac{3}{12}$

27) $\dfrac{4}{13} - \dfrac{1}{13}$

28) $\dfrac{15}{16} - \dfrac{13}{16}$

29) $\dfrac{25}{55} - \dfrac{20}{55}$

30) $\dfrac{10}{23} - \dfrac{7}{23}$

Compare Fractions with Like Denominators

Evaluate and compare. Write < or > or =.

1) $\dfrac{1}{2} + \dfrac{2}{2} \underline{\quad} \dfrac{1}{2}$

2) $\dfrac{3}{4} + \dfrac{1}{4} \underline{\quad} \dfrac{3}{4}$

3) $\dfrac{5}{9} - \dfrac{3}{9} \underline{\quad} \dfrac{6}{9}$

4) $\dfrac{9}{12} + \dfrac{7}{12} \underline{\quad} \dfrac{5}{12}$

5) $\dfrac{5}{7} - \dfrac{3}{7} \underline{\quad} \dfrac{5}{7}$

6) $\dfrac{9}{11} - \dfrac{4}{11} \underline{\quad} \dfrac{3}{11}$

7) $\dfrac{3}{7} + \dfrac{1}{7} \underline{\quad} \dfrac{1}{7}$

8) $\dfrac{11}{10} + \dfrac{4}{10} \underline{\quad} \dfrac{9}{10}$

9) $\dfrac{15}{18} - \dfrac{3}{18} \underline{\quad} \dfrac{15}{18}$

10) $\dfrac{17}{22} + \dfrac{5}{22} \underline{\quad} \dfrac{19}{22}$

11) $\dfrac{14}{18} - \dfrac{4}{18} \underline{\quad} \dfrac{12}{18}$

12) $\dfrac{27}{35} - \dfrac{11}{35} \underline{\quad} \dfrac{20}{35}$

13) $\dfrac{35}{40} + \dfrac{5}{40} \underline{\quad} \dfrac{18}{40}$

14) $\dfrac{25}{29} - \dfrac{3}{29} \underline{\quad} \dfrac{9}{29}$

15) $\dfrac{42}{49} - \dfrac{15}{49} \underline{\quad} \dfrac{30}{49}$

16) $\dfrac{32}{38} + \dfrac{15}{38} \underline{\quad} \dfrac{18}{38}$

More Than Two Fractions with Like Denominators

✍ *Add fractions.*

1) $\dfrac{5}{9} + \dfrac{3}{9} + \dfrac{1}{9}$

2) $\dfrac{2}{7} + \dfrac{4}{7} + \dfrac{1}{7}$

3) $\dfrac{3}{8} + \dfrac{1}{8} + \dfrac{3}{8}$

4) $\dfrac{1}{5} + \dfrac{1}{5} + \dfrac{1}{5}$

5) $\dfrac{5}{17} + \dfrac{3}{17} + \dfrac{4}{17}$

6) $\dfrac{3}{16} + \dfrac{4}{16} + \dfrac{3}{16}$

7) $\dfrac{4}{12} + \dfrac{2}{12} + \dfrac{1}{12}$

8) $\dfrac{5}{19} + \dfrac{5}{19} + \dfrac{3}{19}$

9) $\dfrac{5}{31} + \dfrac{11}{31} + \dfrac{3}{31}$

10) $\dfrac{2}{15} + \dfrac{5}{15} + \dfrac{8}{15}$

11) $\dfrac{3}{35} + \dfrac{4}{35} + \dfrac{4}{35}$

12) $\dfrac{11}{20} + \dfrac{8}{20} + \dfrac{2}{20}$

13) $\dfrac{8}{35} + \dfrac{7}{35} + \dfrac{6}{35}$

14) $\dfrac{19}{28} + \dfrac{12}{28} + \dfrac{11}{28}$

15) $\dfrac{7}{32} + \dfrac{14}{32} + \dfrac{3}{32}$

16) $\dfrac{2}{24} + \dfrac{7}{24} + \dfrac{3}{24}$

Unlike Denominators

✎ *Add fraction.*

1) $\dfrac{3}{5} + \dfrac{1}{7}$

2) $\dfrac{5}{8} + \dfrac{1}{2}$

3) $\dfrac{3}{4} + \dfrac{2}{9}$

4) $\dfrac{2}{6} + \dfrac{1}{3}$

5) $\dfrac{2}{7} + \dfrac{1}{3}$

6) $\dfrac{3}{4} + \dfrac{2}{3}$

7) $\dfrac{16}{15} + \dfrac{3}{10}$

8) $\dfrac{3}{7} + \dfrac{1}{2}$

9) $\dfrac{3}{11} + \dfrac{2}{7}$

10) $\dfrac{1}{3} + \dfrac{1}{18}$

11) $\dfrac{2}{7} + \dfrac{1}{2}$

12) $\dfrac{5}{12} + \dfrac{2}{6}$

13) $\dfrac{3}{8} + \dfrac{1}{4}$

14) $\dfrac{3}{4} + \dfrac{2}{7}$

15) $\dfrac{5}{8} + \dfrac{2}{6}$

16) $\dfrac{2}{7} + \dfrac{1}{3}$

17) $\dfrac{3}{4} + \dfrac{2}{5}$

18) $\dfrac{2}{7} + \dfrac{1}{5}$

19) $\dfrac{1}{3} + \dfrac{1}{7}$

20) $\dfrac{17}{21} + \dfrac{5}{7}$

✎ Subtract fractions.

1) $\dfrac{4}{7} - \dfrac{1}{3}$

2) $\dfrac{3}{5} - \dfrac{1}{6}$

3) $\dfrac{1}{3} - \dfrac{1}{4}$

4) $\dfrac{8}{8} - \dfrac{3}{5}$

5) $\dfrac{3}{7} - \dfrac{3}{21}$

6) $\dfrac{4}{20} - \dfrac{1}{10}$

7) $\dfrac{13}{18} - \dfrac{2}{6}$

8) $\dfrac{5}{8} - \dfrac{2}{4}$

9) $\dfrac{13}{20} - \dfrac{1}{5}$

10) $\dfrac{1}{3} - \dfrac{1}{21}$

11) $\dfrac{4}{9} - \dfrac{2}{7}$

12) $\dfrac{1}{2} - \dfrac{2}{7}$

13) $\dfrac{1}{3} - \dfrac{1}{4}$

14) $\dfrac{5}{6} - \dfrac{1}{4}$

15) $\dfrac{2}{7} - \dfrac{2}{21}$

16) $\dfrac{1}{5} - \dfrac{4}{25}$

17) $\dfrac{17}{16} - \dfrac{3}{4}$

18) $\dfrac{3}{8} - \dfrac{1}{3}$

19) $\dfrac{13}{24} - \dfrac{5}{12}$

20) $\dfrac{3}{5} - \dfrac{4}{11}$

Ordering Fractions

✍ *Order the fractions from least to greatest.*

1) $\dfrac{1}{4}, \dfrac{1}{3}, \dfrac{1}{5}, \dfrac{1}{2}$ _____, _____, _____, _____

2) $\dfrac{3}{4}, \dfrac{1}{6}, \dfrac{3}{8}, \dfrac{1}{12}$ _____, _____, _____, _____

3) $\dfrac{5}{7}, \dfrac{2}{7}, \dfrac{12}{14}, \dfrac{5}{14}$ _____, _____, _____, _____

4) $\dfrac{2}{3}, \dfrac{5}{6}, \dfrac{4}{9}, \dfrac{7}{18}$ _____, _____, _____, _____

5) $\dfrac{1}{5}, \dfrac{1}{15}, \dfrac{1}{11}, \dfrac{1}{8}$ _____, _____, _____, _____

✍ *Order the fractions from greatest to least.*

6) $\dfrac{2}{5}, \dfrac{3}{7}, \dfrac{4}{9}, \dfrac{5}{11}$ _____, _____, _____, _____

7) $\dfrac{6}{10}, \dfrac{4}{5}, \dfrac{2}{3}, \dfrac{1}{2}$ _____, _____, _____, _____

8) $\dfrac{3}{7}, \dfrac{1}{6}, \dfrac{4}{15}, \dfrac{2}{4}$ _____, _____, _____, _____

9) $\dfrac{5}{6}, \dfrac{3}{4}, \dfrac{9}{16}, \dfrac{11}{12}$ _____, _____, _____, _____

10) $\dfrac{15}{32}, \dfrac{13}{24}, \dfrac{5}{28}, \dfrac{15}{16}$ _____, _____, _____, _____

Denominators of 10, 100, and 1000

✐ *Add fractions.*

1) $\dfrac{6}{10} + \dfrac{30}{100}$

2) $\dfrac{5}{10} + \dfrac{30}{100}$

3) $\dfrac{26}{100} + \dfrac{4}{10}$

4) $\dfrac{63}{100} + \dfrac{1}{10}$

5) $\dfrac{23}{100} + \dfrac{2}{10}$

6) $\dfrac{2}{10} + \dfrac{40}{100}$

7) $\dfrac{70}{100} + \dfrac{1}{10}$

8) $\dfrac{30}{100} + \dfrac{3}{10}$

9) $\dfrac{56}{100} + \dfrac{3}{10}$

10) $\dfrac{5}{10} + \dfrac{12}{100}$

11) $\dfrac{9}{10} + \dfrac{10}{100}$

12) $\dfrac{20}{100} + \dfrac{3}{10}$

13) $\dfrac{43}{100} + \dfrac{3}{10}$

14) $\dfrac{21}{100} + \dfrac{6}{10}$

15) $\dfrac{35}{100} + \dfrac{2}{10}$

16) $\dfrac{1}{10} + \dfrac{81}{100}$

17) $\dfrac{15}{100} + \dfrac{5}{10}$

18) $\dfrac{26}{100} + \dfrac{7}{10}$

✎ Subtract fractions.

1) $\dfrac{8}{10} - \dfrac{20}{100}$

2) $\dfrac{5}{10} - \dfrac{27}{100}$

3) $\dfrac{25}{100} - \dfrac{150}{1000}$

4) $\dfrac{71}{100} - \dfrac{320}{1000}$

5) $\dfrac{23}{100} - \dfrac{180}{1000}$

6) $\dfrac{30}{10} - \dfrac{780}{1000}$

7) $\dfrac{70}{100} - \dfrac{560}{1000}$

8) $\dfrac{78}{100} - \dfrac{5}{10}$

9) $\dfrac{850}{1000} - \dfrac{6}{10}$

10) $\dfrac{64}{100} - \dfrac{240}{1000}$

11) $\dfrac{7}{10} - \dfrac{15}{100}$

12) $\dfrac{75}{100} - \dfrac{6}{10}$

13) $\dfrac{70}{100} - \dfrac{5}{10}$

14) $\dfrac{800}{1000} - \dfrac{5}{100}$

15) $\dfrac{300}{1000} - \dfrac{20}{100}$

16) $\dfrac{870}{1000} - \dfrac{6}{10}$

17) $\dfrac{50}{100} - \dfrac{4}{10}$

18) $\dfrac{60}{100} - \dfrac{150}{1000}$

Fractions to Mixed Numbers

Convert fractions to mixed numbers.

1) $\dfrac{11}{4}$

2) $\dfrac{39}{5}$

3) $\dfrac{33}{6}$

4) $\dfrac{32}{10}$

5) $\dfrac{13}{2}$

6) $\dfrac{66}{10}$

7) $\dfrac{20}{8}$

8) $\dfrac{8}{5}$

9) $\dfrac{17}{5}$

10) $\dfrac{26}{10}$

11) $\dfrac{8}{6}$

12) $\dfrac{14}{8}$

13) $\dfrac{9}{2}$

14) $\dfrac{41}{4}$

15) $\dfrac{62}{10}$

16) $\dfrac{11}{3}$

17) $\dfrac{43}{8}$

18) $\dfrac{24}{5}$

Mixed Numbers to Fractions

✎ *Convert to fraction.*

1) $1\frac{2}{7}$

2) $2\frac{3}{5}$

3) $5\frac{1}{4}$

4) $6\frac{4}{7}$

5) $3\frac{1}{4}$

6) $2\frac{3}{7}$

7) $3\frac{4}{9}$

8) $4\frac{9}{10}$

9) $6\frac{5}{6}$

10) $6\frac{10}{11}$

11) $4\frac{9}{20}$

12) $8\frac{2}{7}$

13) $5\frac{3}{5}$

14) $5\frac{1}{6}$

15) $8\frac{3}{4}$

16) $10\frac{2}{5}$

17) $10\frac{3}{7}$

18) $12\frac{6}{7}$

Add and Subtract Mixed Numbers

✍ Add mixed numbers.

1) $4\frac{2}{3} + 5\frac{1}{2}$

7) $5\frac{3}{7} - 1\frac{5}{7}$

2) $4\frac{1}{2} + 6\frac{4}{5}$

8) $5\frac{6}{5} - 2\frac{8}{15}$

3) $4\frac{1}{5} + 6\frac{1}{2}$

9) $5\frac{21}{25} - 1\frac{12}{25}$

4) $3\frac{1}{2} + 6\frac{1}{3}$

10) $5\frac{2}{8} + 3\frac{1}{2}$

5) $4\frac{1}{3} - 1\frac{2}{3}$

11) $3\frac{5}{8} + 2\frac{1}{8}$

6) $6\frac{3}{15} - 1\frac{3}{5}$

12) $6\frac{2}{7} + 2\frac{1}{5}$

Answers of Worksheets – Chapter 4

Simplifying Fractions

1) $\frac{11}{21}$

2) $\frac{2}{5}$

3) $\frac{3}{4}$

4) $\frac{1}{6}$

5) $\frac{1}{2}$

6) $\frac{1}{7}$

7) $\frac{2}{7}$

8) $\frac{1}{3}$

9) $\frac{4}{5}$

10) $\frac{1}{7}$

11) $\frac{1}{3}$

12) $\frac{3}{2}$

13) $\frac{5}{7}$

14) $\frac{3}{4}$

15) $\frac{1}{5}$

16) $\frac{5}{8}$

17) $\frac{3}{8}$

18) $\frac{3}{8}$

19) $\frac{1}{9}$

20) $\frac{3}{4}$

Add Fractions with Like Denominators

1) 1

2) 1

3) $\frac{11}{8}$

4) $\frac{6}{5}$

5) $\frac{7}{12}$

6) $\frac{5}{8}$

7) $\frac{8}{7}$

8) $\frac{12}{13}$

9) $\frac{17}{18}$

10) $\frac{13}{12}$

11) $\frac{10}{16}$

12) $\frac{17}{25}$

13) 1

14) $\frac{12}{20}$

15) $\frac{12}{13}$

16) $\frac{33}{35}$

17) $\frac{23}{27}$

18) $\frac{13}{15}$

19) $\frac{33}{42}$

20) $\frac{23}{33}$

21) $\frac{25}{30}$

22) 1

23) $\frac{5}{8}$

24) $\frac{7}{9}$

25) $\frac{7}{10}$

26) $\frac{8}{10}$

27) $\frac{6}{7}$

28) 1

29) $\frac{2}{11}$

30) $\frac{17}{25}$

Subtract Fractions with Like Denominators

1) $\frac{4}{7}$

2) $\frac{3}{5}$

3) $\frac{1}{11}$

4) $\frac{5}{8}$

5) $\frac{4}{10}$

6) $\frac{5}{7}$

7) $\frac{2}{9}$

8) $\frac{1}{15}$

9) $\frac{3}{13}$

10) $\frac{1}{12}$ 17) $\frac{5}{37}$ 24) $\frac{1}{4}$

11) $\frac{6}{24}$ 18) $\frac{10}{26}$ 25) $\frac{5}{10}$

12) $\frac{2}{21}$ 19) $\frac{20}{45}$ 26) $\frac{1}{4}$

13) $\frac{1}{27}$ 20) $\frac{1}{3}$ 27) $\frac{3}{13}$

14) $\frac{8}{36}$ 21) $\frac{10}{38}$ 28) $\frac{2}{16}$

15) $\frac{11}{27}$ 22) $\frac{1}{5}$ 29) $\frac{1}{11}$

16) $\frac{12}{45}$ 23) $\frac{2}{7}$ 30) $\frac{3}{23}$

Compare Fractions with Like Denominators

1) $\frac{3}{2} > \frac{1}{2}$ 7) $\frac{4}{7} > \frac{1}{7}$ 13) $1 > \frac{18}{40}$

2) $1 > \frac{3}{4}$ 8) $\frac{15}{10} > \frac{9}{10}$ 14) $\frac{22}{29} > \frac{9}{29}$

3) $\frac{2}{9} < \frac{6}{9}$ 9) $\frac{12}{18} < \frac{15}{18}$ 15) $\frac{27}{49} < \frac{30}{49}$

4) $\frac{16}{12} > \frac{5}{12}$ 10) $1 > \frac{19}{22}$ 16) $\frac{47}{38} > \frac{18}{38}$

5) $\frac{2}{7} < \frac{5}{7}$ 11) $\frac{10}{18} < \frac{12}{18}$

6) $\frac{5}{11} > \frac{3}{11}$ 12) $\frac{16}{35} < \frac{20}{35}$

More Than Two Fractions with Like Denominators

1) 1 5) $\frac{12}{17}$ 9) $\frac{19}{31}$ 13) $\frac{21}{35}$

2) 1 6) $\frac{10}{16}$ 10) 1 14) $\frac{3}{2}$

3) $\frac{7}{8}$ 7) $\frac{7}{12}$ 11) $\frac{11}{35}$ 15) $\frac{3}{4}$

4) $\frac{3}{5}$ 8) $\frac{13}{19}$ 12) $\frac{21}{20}$ 16) $\frac{12}{24}$

Add fractions with unlike denominators

1) $\frac{26}{35}$

2) $\frac{9}{8}$

3) $\frac{35}{36}$

4) $\frac{2}{3}$

5) $\frac{13}{21}$

6) $\frac{17}{12}$

7) $\frac{205}{150}$

8) $\frac{13}{14}$

9) $\frac{43}{77}$

10) $\frac{7}{18}$

11) $\frac{6}{7}$

12) $\frac{3}{4}$

13) $\frac{5}{8}$

14) $\frac{29}{28}$

15) $\frac{23}{24}$

16) $\frac{13}{21}$

17) $\frac{23}{20}$

18) $\frac{17}{35}$

19) $\frac{10}{21}$

20) $\frac{32}{21}$

Subtract fractions with unlike denominators

1) $\frac{5}{21}$

2) $\frac{13}{30}$

3) $\frac{1}{12}$

4) $\frac{2}{5}$

5) $\frac{6}{21}$

6) $\frac{1}{10}$

7) $\frac{7}{18}$

8) $\frac{1}{8}$

9) $\frac{9}{20}$

10) $\frac{6}{21}$

11) $\frac{10}{63}$

12) $\frac{3}{14}$

13) $\frac{1}{12}$

14) $\frac{7}{12}$

15) $\frac{4}{21}$

16) $\frac{1}{5}$

17) $\frac{5}{16}$

18) $\frac{1}{24}$

19) $\frac{1}{8}$

20) $\frac{13}{55}$

Ordering Fractions

1) $\frac{1}{5}, \frac{1}{4}, \frac{1}{3}, \frac{1}{2}$

2) $\frac{1}{12}, \frac{1}{6}, \frac{3}{8}, \frac{3}{4},$

3) $\frac{2}{7}, \frac{5}{14}, \frac{5}{7}, \frac{12}{14}$

4) $\frac{7}{18}, \frac{4}{9}, \frac{2}{3}, \frac{5}{6}$

5) $\frac{1}{5}, \frac{1}{8}, \frac{1}{11}, \frac{1}{15}$

6) $\frac{5}{11}, \frac{4}{9}, \frac{3}{7}, \frac{2}{5}$

7) $\frac{4}{5}, \frac{2}{3}, \frac{6}{10}, \frac{1}{2}$

8) $\frac{2}{4}, \frac{3}{7}, \frac{4}{15}, \frac{1}{6}$

9) $\frac{11}{12}, \frac{5}{6}, \frac{3}{4}, \frac{9}{16}$

10) $\frac{15}{16}, \frac{13}{24}, \frac{15}{32}, \frac{5}{28}$

Add fractions with denominators of 10, 100, and 1000

1) $\frac{9}{10}$

2) $\frac{4}{5}$

3) $\frac{33}{50}$

4) $\frac{73}{100}$

5) $\frac{43}{100}$

6) $\frac{3}{5}$

7) $\frac{4}{5}$

8) $\frac{3}{5}$

9) $\frac{43}{50}$

10) $\frac{31}{50}$

11) 1

12) $\frac{1}{2}$

13) $\frac{73}{100}$ 15) $\frac{11}{20}$ 17) $\frac{65}{100}$

14) $\frac{81}{100}$ 16) $\frac{91}{100}$ 18) $\frac{24}{25}$

Subtract fractions with denominators of 10, 100, and 1000

1) $\frac{60}{100}$ 6) $\frac{111}{50}$ 11) $\frac{11}{20}$ 16) $\frac{27}{100}$

2) $\frac{23}{100}$ 7) $\frac{7}{50}$ 12) $\frac{3}{20}$ 17) $\frac{1}{10}$

3) $\frac{1}{10}$ 8) $\frac{14}{50}$ 13) $\frac{1}{50}$ 18) $\frac{9}{20}$

4) $\frac{39}{100}$ 9) $\frac{1}{4}$ 14) $\frac{75}{100}$

5) $\frac{1}{20}$ 10) $\frac{1}{25}$ 15) $\frac{1}{10}$

Fractions to Mixed Numbers

1) $2\frac{3}{4}$ 6) $6\frac{3}{5}$ 11) $1\frac{1}{3}$ 16) $3\frac{2}{3}$

2) $7\frac{4}{5}$ 7) $2\frac{1}{2}$ 12) $1\frac{3}{4}$ 17) $5\frac{3}{8}$

3) $5\frac{1}{2}$ 8) $1\frac{3}{5}$ 13) $4\frac{1}{2}$ 18) $4\frac{4}{5}$

4) $3\frac{1}{5}$ 9) $3\frac{2}{5}$ 14) $10\frac{1}{4}$

5) $6\frac{1}{2}$ 10) $2\frac{3}{5}$ 15) $6\frac{1}{5}$

Mixed Numbers to Fractions

1) $\frac{9}{7}$ 6) $\frac{17}{7}$ 11) $\frac{89}{20}$ 16) $\frac{52}{5}$

2) $\frac{13}{5}$ 7) $\frac{31}{9}$ 12) $\frac{58}{7}$ 17) $\frac{73}{7}$

3) $\frac{21}{4}$ 8) $\frac{49}{10}$ 13) $\frac{28}{5}$ 18) $\frac{90}{7}$

4) $\frac{46}{7}$ 9) $\frac{41}{6}$ 14) $\frac{31}{6}$

5) $\frac{13}{4}$ 10) $\frac{76}{11}$ 15) $\frac{35}{4}$

Add and Subtract Mixed Numbers with Like Denominators

1) $10\ \frac{1}{6}$

2) $11\frac{3}{10}$

3) $10\frac{7}{10}$

4) $9\frac{5}{6}$

5) $2\frac{2}{3}$

6) $4\frac{9}{15}$

7) $3\frac{5}{7}$

8) $3\frac{10}{15}$

9) $4\frac{9}{25}$

10) $8\frac{6}{8}$

11) $5\frac{7}{8}$

12) $8\frac{17}{35}$

Chapter 5: Decimal

Topics that you'll learn in this chapter:

- ✓ Decimal Place Value
- ✓ Ordering and Comparing Decimals
- ✓ Decimal Addition
- ✓ Decimal Subtraction

Decimal Place Value

What place is the selected digit?

1) 5,13<u>2</u>.25

2) 5,621.3<u>2</u>

3) 4,2<u>5</u>8.91

4) 8,47<u>2</u>.66

5) 9,235.<u>6</u>3

6) 5,6<u>6</u>3.24

7) <u>1</u>,654.49

8) 5,758.<u>7</u>4

9) 7,<u>9</u>35.66

10) 2,24<u>9</u>.21

What is the value of the selected digit?

11) 4,325.<u>3</u>2

12) 1,31<u>8</u>.66

13) 6,352.25

14) <u>3</u>,736.16

15) 4,9<u>3</u>6.78

16) 9,62<u>5</u>.86

17) 8,3<u>1</u>3.45

18) <u>2</u>,168.82

19) 3,<u>4</u>36.76

20) 2,143.2<u>3</u>

Ordering and Comparing Decimals

Use > = <.

1) 0.25 __ 0. 36

2) 0.33 __ 0.38

3) 0.66 __ 0.49

4) 0.56 __ 0.58

5) 0.67 __ 0. 76

6) 0.8 __ 0.68

7) 0.95 __ 7.55

8) 0.53 __ 0.77

9) 0.5 __ 0.23

10) 0.7 __ 0.3

11) 0.77 __ 0.6

12) 0.9 __ 0.90

✎ Order each set of integers from least to greatest.

13) 0.5, 0.57, 0.24, 0.77, 0.35   ___, ___, ___, ___, ___, ___

14) 1.4, 3.4, 1.87, 2.65, 1.90   ___, ___, ___, ___, ___, ___

15) 2.5, 1.2, 1.9, 0.65, 0.32   ___, ___, ___, ___, ___, ___

16) 1.6, 1.2, 2.2, 4.2, 1.34, 2.55   ___, ___, ___, ___, ___, ___

Decimal Addition

✎ Add.

1) 7.12 + 4.24 =

2) 2.5 + 1.6 =

3) 7.2 + 1.34 =

4) 3.4 + 1.57 =

5) 2.55 + 6.25 =

6) 5.87 + 4.30 =

7) 13.45 + 14.25 =

8) 13.45 + 11.31 =

9) 18.25 + 12.34 =

10) 15.25 + 12.55 =

11) 21.25 + 22.90 =

12) 15.25 + 12.88 =

13) 19.44 + 15.65 =

14) 33.2 + 20.45 =

15) 12.72 + 16.68 =

16) 20.25 + 23.75 =

17) 30.95 + 23.40 =

18) 25.6 + 26.6 =

Decimal Subtraction

✎ *Subtract.*

1) $5.3 - 3.67 =$

2) $5.87 - 3.32 =$

3) $9.25 - 6.55 =$

4) $5.34 - 2.12 =$

5) $6.05 - 1.27 =$

6) $3.15 - 2.55 =$

7) $57.62 - 4.35 =$

8) $4.24 - 2.75 =$

9) $17.5 - 15.11 =$

10) $16.56 - 11.32 =$

11) $15.78 - 12.25 =$

12) $14.2 - 12.4 =$

13) $25.14 - 18.2 =$

14) $29.8 - 23.2 =$

15) $19.55 - 8.12 =$

16) $23.25 - 20.4 =$

17) $32.34 - 26.21 =$

18) $34.34 - 25.5 =$

Answers of Worksheets – Chapter 5

Decimal Place Value

1) one	8) tenths	15) 30
2) hundredths	9) hundreds	16) 5
3) tens	10) ones	17) 10
4) one	11) 0.1	18) 2,000
5) tenths	12) 8	19) 400
6) tens	13) 0.05	20) 0.03
7) thousands	14) 3000	

Order and Comparing Decimals

1) <	5) <	9) >
2) <	6) >	10) >
3) >	7) <	11) >
4) <	8) <	12) =

13) 0.24, 0.35, 0.5, 0.57, 0.77

14) 1.4, 1.87, 1.90, 2.65, 3.4

15) 0.32, 0.65, 1.2, 1.9, 2.5

16) 1.2, 1.34, 1.6, 2.2, 2.55, 4.2

Decimal Addition

1) 11.36	7) 27.7	13) 35.09
2) 4.1	8) 24.76	14) 53.65
3) 8.54	9) 30.59	15) 29.4
4) 4.97	10) 27.80	16) 44
5) 8.80	11) 44.15	17) 54.35
6) 10.17	12) 28.13	18) 52.2

Decimal Subtraction

1- 1.63	7- 53.27	13- 6.94
2- 2.55	8- 1.49	14- 6.6
3- 2.7	9- 2.39	15- 11.43
4- 3.22	10- 5.24	16- 2.85
5- 4.78	11- 3.53	17- 6.13
6- 0.6	12- 1.8	18- 8.84

Chapter 6: Algebra

Topics that you'll learn in this chapter:

- ✓ Find a Rule between input and output
- ✓ Find Output Using Equation
- ✓ Find Input Using Equation

Find a Rule

✍Complete the output.

1- **Rule:** the output is $x - 12$

Input	x	18	25	32	39	46
Output	y					

2- **Rule:** the output is $x \times 24$

Input	x	4	6	8	10	12
Output	y					

3- **Rule:** the output is $x \div 9$

Input	x	180	162	144	126	108
Output	y					

✍Find a rule to write an expression.

4- **Rule:** _____

Input	x	12	14	16	18
Output	y	48	56	64	72

5- **Rule:** _____

Input	x	14	26	38	50
Output	y	20	32	44	56

6- **Rule:** _____

Input	x	154	168	182	196
Output	y	22	24	26	28

Output

✍ *Write output of each algebraic expression.*

1) $9 - x, x = 2$

2) $x + 2, x = 4$

3) $3x + 7, x = 2$

4) $x + (-5), x = -3$

5) $3x + 6, x = 2$

6) $4x + 6, x = -2$

7) $10 + 2x - 6, x = 2$

8) $10 - 3x, x = 7$

9) $\frac{30}{x} - 3, x = 6$

10) $(-3) + \frac{x}{4} + 2x, x = 8$

11) $(-2) + \frac{x}{7}, x = 42$

12) $\left(-\frac{14}{x}\right) - 3 + 4x, x = 2$

13) $\left(-\frac{9}{x}\right) - 9 + 2x, x = 3$

14) $(-4) + \frac{x}{4}, x = 16$

15) $5(5x - 10), x = -1$

16) $2x + 4x - 3 + 2,$

   $x = 1$

17) $\left(-\frac{12}{x}\right) + 1 + 5x,$

   $x = 4$

18) $2(2a + 5a),$

   $a = 3$

19) $10 + 3x + 7 - 2x,$

   $x = 5$

20) $9x - 6 - 4x,$

   $x = 2$

21) $2 + 3(2x + x),$

   $x = 1$

22) $10x + x - 3x,$

   $x = 3$

23) $x \times 9 \div x,$

   $x = 6$

Input

✏️ *Write input of each algebraic expression.*

1) $x + 3 = 12$

2) $20 = (-5) + x$

3) $4x = 40$

4) $36 = 4x$

5) $(-6) = 5 + x$

6) $2 + x = (-3)$

7) $20x = 240$

8) $20 = x + 5$

9) $(-26) + x = (-10)$

10) $9x = 45$

11) $x - 13 = (-26)$

12) $x - 3 = (-15)$

13) $(-30) = x - 25$

14) $16 = 2x$

15) $6x = 24$

16) $66 = 6x$

17) $x - 40 = 20$

18) $8x = 64$

19) $32 = 4x$

20) $4x = 72$

21) $x + 28 = 40$

22) $x - 5 = 31$

23) $34 + x - 21 = 0$

24) $40x = 400$

Answers of Worksheets – Chapter 6

Find a Rule

1)

Input	x	18	25	32	39	46
Output	y	30	37	44	51	58

2)

Input	x	4	6	8	10	12
Output	y	96	144	192	240	288

3)

Input	x	18	25	32	39	46
Output	y	20	18	16	14	12

4) $y = 4x$

5) $y = x + 6$

6) $y = x \div 7$

Output

1) 7	7) 8	13) −6	19) 22
2) 6	8) −11	14) 0	20) 4
3) 13	9) 2	15) −75	21) 14
4) −8	10) 15	16) 5	22) 24
5) 12	11) 4	17) 18	23) 9
6) −2	12) −2	18) 42	

Input

1) 9	7) 12	13) − 5	19) 8
2) 25	8) 15	14) 8	20) 18
3) 10	9) 16	15) 4	21) 12
4) 9	10) 5	16) 11	22) 36
5) − 11	11) − 13	17) 60	23) −13
6) − 5	12) − 12	18) 8	24) 10

Chapter 7: Measurement

Topics that you'll learn in this chapter:

- ✓ Reference Measurement
- ✓ Metric Length
- ✓ Customary Length
- ✓ Metric Capacity
- ✓ Customary Capacity
- ✓ Metric Weight and Mass
- ✓ Customary Weight and Mass
- ✓ Time
- ✓ Add Money Amounts
- ✓ Subtract Money Amounts
- ✓ Money: Word Problems

Reference Measurement

LENGTH

Customary	Metric
1 mile (mi) = 1,760 yards (yd)	1 kilometer (km) = 1,000 meters (m)
1 yard (yd) = 3 feet (ft)	1 meter (m) = 100 centimeters (cm)
1 foot (ft) = 12 inches (in.)	1 centimeter(cm) = 10 millimeters(mm)

VOLUME AND CAPACITY

Customary	Metric
1 gallon (gal) = 4 quarts (qt)	1 liter (L) = 1,000 milliliters (mL)
1 quart (qt) = 2 pints (pt.)	
1 pint (pt.) = 2 cups (c)	
1 cup (c) = 8 fluid ounces (Fl oz)	

WEIGHT AND MASS

Customary	Metric
1 ton (T) = 2,000 pounds (lb.)	1 kilogram (kg) = 1,000 grams (g)
1 pound (lb.) = 16 ounces (oz)	1 gram (g) = 1,000 milligrams (mg)

Time

1 year = 12 months

1 year = 52 weeks

1 week = 7 days

1 day = 24 hours

1 hour = 60 minutes

1 minute = 60 seconds

Metric Length Measurement

✏️*Convert to the units.*

1) 20 mm = _____ cm

2) 2 m = _____ mm

3) 3 m = _____ cm

4) 4 km = _____ m

5) 7,000 mm = _____ m

6) 600 cm = _____ m

7) 10 m = _____ cm

8) 1,000 mm = _____ cm

9) 5,000 mm = _____ m

10) 3 km = _____ mm

11) 10 km = _____ m

12) 20 m = _____ cm

13) 3,000 m = _____ km

14) 6,000 m = _____ km

Customary Length Measurement

✏️*Convert to the units.*

1) 5 ft = _____ in

2) 2 ft = _____ in

3) 2 yd = _____ ft

4) 4 yd = _____ ft

5) 2 yd = _____ in

6) 24 in = _____ ft

7) 216 in = _____ yd

8) 108 in = _____ yd

9) 19 yd = _____ in

10) 68 yd = _____ in

11) 87 ft = _____ yd

12) 120 ft = _____ yd

13) 72 in = _____ ft

14) 56 yd = _____ feet

Metric Capacity Measurement

✍ *Convert the following measurements.*

1) 20 l = _____ ml

2) 5 l = _____ ml

3) 30 l = _____ ml

4) 22 l = _____ ml

5) 24 l = _____ ml

6) 16 l = _____ ml

7) 60,000 l = _____ l

8) 42,000m ml = _____ l

9) 96,000 ml = _____ l

10) 2000 ml = _____ l

11) 9000 ml = _____ l

12) 80, 000 ml = _____ l

Customary Capacity Measurement

✍ *Convert the following measurements.*

1) 76 gal = _____ qt.

2) 43 gal = _____ pt.

3) 82 gal = _____ c.

4) 14 pt. = _____ c

5) 19 qt = _____ pt.

6) 17 qt = _____ c

7) 28 pt. = _____ c

8) 72 c = _____ gal

9) 152 pt. = _____ gal

10) 128 qt = _____ gal

11) 162 pt. = _____ qt

12) 96 c = _____ qt

13) 158 c = _____ pt.

14) 232 qt = _____ gal

15) 136 pt. = _____ qt

16) 68 gal = _____ pt.

Metric Weight and Mass Measurement

✐ *Convert.*

1) 30 kg = _____ g

2) 55 kg = _____ g

3) 200 kg = _____ g

4) 40 kg = _____ g

5) 65 kg = _____ g

6) 90 kg = _____ g

7) 38 kg = _____ g

8) 82,000 g = _____ kg

9) 630,000 g = _____ kg

10) 200,000 g = _____ kg

11) 50,000 g = _____ kg

12) 10,000 g = _____ kg

13) 650,000 g = _____ kg

14) 100,000 g = _____ kg

Customary Weight and Mass Measurement

✐ *Convert.*

1) 4,000 lb. = _____ T

2) 10,000 lb. = _____ T

3) 2,000 lb. = _____ T

4) 16,000 lb. = _____ T

5) 35 lb. = _____ oz

6) 56 lb. = _____ oz

7) 140 lb. = _____ oz

8) 3 T = _____ lb.

9) 8 T = _____ lb.

10) 11 T = _____ lb.

11) 25 T = _____ lb.

12) 9 T = _____ oz

13) 5 T = _____ oz

14) 12 T = _____ oz

Time

✍ Convert to the units.

1) 30 hr = _____ min

8) 30 day = _____ hr

2) 12 year = _____ week

9) 1 day = _____ min

3) 5 hr = _____ sec

10) 360 min = _____ hr

4) 75 min = _____ sec

11) 30 year = _____ month

5) 1200 min = _____ hr

12) 3600 sec = _____ min

6) 730 day = _____ year

13) 168 hr = _____ day

7) 1 year = _____ hr

14) 18 weeks = _____ day

✍ How much time has passed?

1) From 2:15 A.M. to 5:25 A.M.: _____ hours and ___ minutes.

2) From 1:20 A.M. to 6:05 A.M.: _____ hours and ___ minutes.

3) It's 7:30 P.M. What time was 4 hours ago? _____ O'clock

4) 2:10 A.M to 5:30 AM: _____ hours and _____ minutes.

5) 3:35 A.M to 6:10 AM: _____ hours and _____ minutes.

6) 7:00 A.M. to 8:25 AM. = _____ hour(s) and _____ minutes.

7) 11:45 A.M. to 4:15 PM. = _____ hour(s) and _____ minutes

8) 6:15 A.M. to 6:50 A.M. = _____ minutes

9) 3:05 A.M. to 3:52 A.M. = _____ minutes

Money Amounts

Add.

1)
$214	$424	$290
+$132	+$510	+$315

2)
$421	$530	$632
+$430	+$421	+$245

3)
$411	$560	$730
+$312	+$228	+$210

4)
$621.60	$321.20	$615.00
+$163.70	+$120.75	+$356.30

Subtract.

5)
$835	$641	$732
−$154	−$110	−$534

6)
$436	$498	$640
−$137	−$326	−$549

7)
$356.40	$710.50	$632.70
−$219.70	−$128.80	−$379.20

8) Linda had $15.00. She bought some game tickets for $8.14.

How much did she have left?

Money: Word Problems

✍ *Solve.*

1) How many boxes of envelopes can you buy with $42 if one box costs $6?

2) After paying $7.15 for a salad, Ella has $42.36. How much money did she have before buying the salad?

3) How many packages of diapers can you buy with $75 if one package costs $5?

4) Last week James ran 40 miles more than Michael. James ran 66 miles. How many miles did Michael run?

5) Last Friday Jacob had $36.52. Over the weekend he received some money for cleaning the attic. He now has $55. How much money did he receive?

6) After paying $12.12 for a sandwich, Amelia has $45.50. How much money did she have before buying the sandwich?

Answers of Worksheets – Chapter 7

Metric length

1) 2 cm	6) 6 m	11) 10,000 m
2) 2000 mm	7) 1000 cm	12) 2,000 cm
3) 300 cm	8) 10 cm	13) 3 km
4) 4000 m	9) 5 m	14) 6 km
5) 7 m	10) 3,000,000 mm	

Customary Length

1) 60	6) 2	11) 29
2) 24	7) 6	12) 40
3) 6	8) 3	13) 6
4) 12	9) 684	14) 168
5) 72	10) 2,488	

Metric Capacity

1) 20,000 ml	5) 24,000 ml	9) 96 ml
2) 5,000 ml	6) 16,000 ml	10) 2L
3) 30,000 ml	7) 60 ml	11) 9 L
4) 22,000 ml	8) 42 ml	12) 80 L

Customary Capacity

1) 304 qt	5) 38 pt.	9) 19 gal	13) 79 pt.
2) 344 pt.	6) 68 c	10) 32 gal	14) 58 gal
3) 1312 c	7) 56 c	11) 81 qt	15) 68 qt
4) 28 c	8) 9 gal	12) 24qt	16) 544 pt.

Metric Weight and Mass

1) 30,000 g	4) 40,000 g	7) 38,000 g
2) 55,000 g	5) 65,000 g	8) 82 kg
3) 200,000 g	6) 90,000 g	9) 630 kg

10) 200 kg   12) 10 kg   14) 100 kg

11) 50 kg   13) 650 kg

Customary Weight and Mass

1) 2 T	6) 896 oz	11) 50,000 lb.
2) 5 T	7) 2,240 oz	12) 288,000 oz
3) 1 T	8) 6,000 lb.	13) 160,000 oz
4) 8 T	9) 16,000 lb.	14) 384,000 oz
5) 560 oz	10) 22,000 lb.	

Time - Convert

1) 1,800 min	6) 2 year	11) 360 months
2) 624 weeks	7) 8,760 hr	12) 60 min
3) 18,000 sec	8) 720 hr	13) 7 days
4) 4,500 sec	9) 1,440 min	14) 126 days
5) 20 hr	10) 6 hr	

Time - Gap

1) 3:10	4) 3:20	7) 4:30
2) 4:45	5) 2:35	8) 35 minutes
3) 3:30 P.M.	6) 1:25	9) 47 minutes

Add Money

1) 346, 934, 605   3) 723, 788, 940

2) 851, 951, 877   4) 785.30, 441.95, 971.30

Subtract Money

5) 681–531–198   7) 136.70–581.70–253.50

6) 299–172–91   8) $6.86

Money: word problem

1) 7	3) 15	5) 18.48
2) $49.51	4) 26	6) 47.62

Chapter 8: Geometric

Topics that you'll learn in this chapter:

- ✓ Identifying Angles: Acute, Right, Obtuse, and Straight Angles
- ✓ Measure Angles with a Protractor
- ✓ Estimate Angle Measurements
- ✓ Polygon Names
- ✓ Classify Triangles
- ✓ Parallel Sides in Quadrilaterals
- ✓ Identify Parallelograms
- ✓ Identify Trapezoids
- ✓ Identify Rectangles
- ✓ Perimeter: Find the Missing Side Lengths
- ✓ Perimeter and Area of Squares
- ✓ Perimeter and Area of rectangles
- ✓ Area and Perimeter: Word Problems
- ✓ Volume of Cubes and Rectangle Prisms

Identifying Angles

Write the name of the angles (Acute, Right, Obtuse, and Straight Angles).

1)

2)

3)

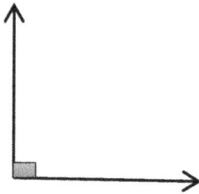

4)

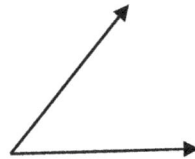

5)

6)

7)

8)

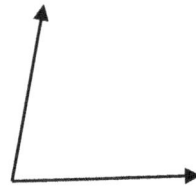

Estimate Angle Measurements

✍️Estimate the approximate measurement of each angle in

degrees.

1)

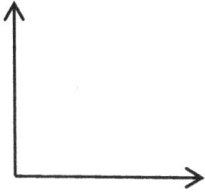

2)

3)

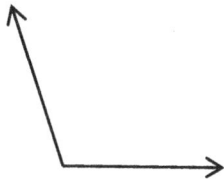

4)

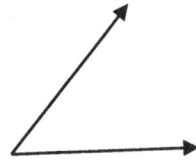

5)

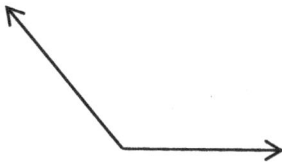

6)

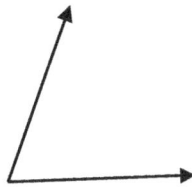

7)

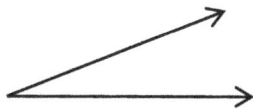

8)

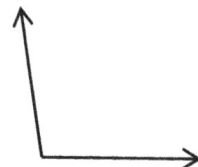

Polygon Names

✎ Write name of polygons.

1)

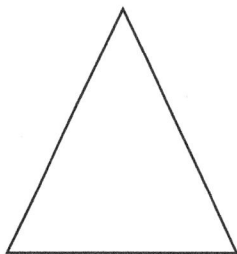

2)

3)

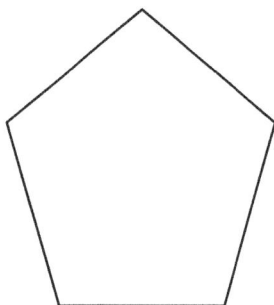

4)

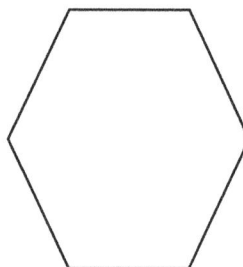

5)

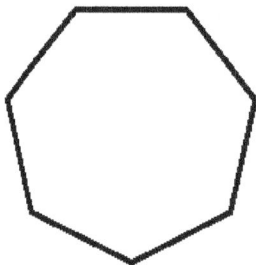

6)

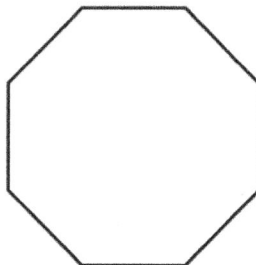

Classify Triangles

✍ Classify the triangles by their sides and angles.

1)

2)

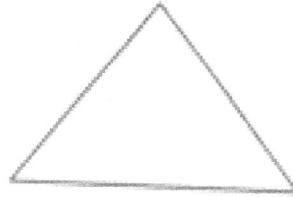

3)

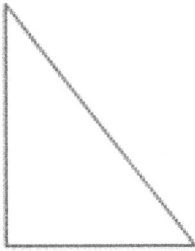

4)

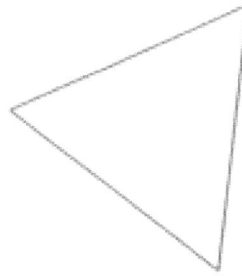

5)

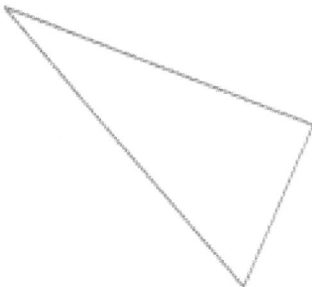

6)

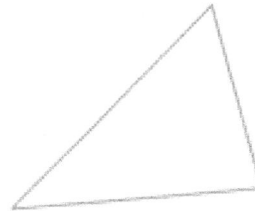

Parallel Sides in Quadrilaterals

✐ *Write name of quadrilaterals.*

1)

2)

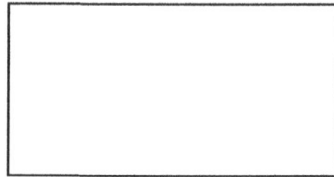

3)

4)

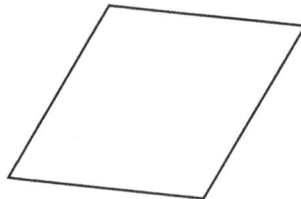

5)

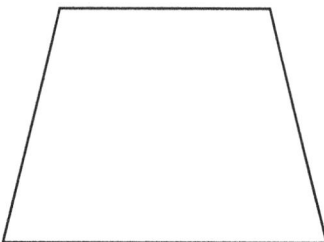

6)

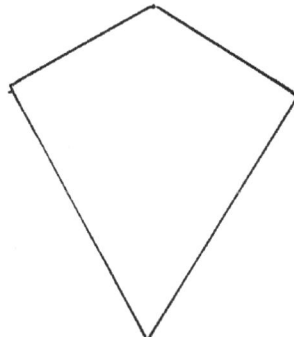

Identify Rectangles

Solve.

1) A rectangle has _____ sides and _____ angles.

2) Draw a rectangle that is 7centimeters long and 3 centimeters wide. What is the perimeter?

3) Draw a rectangle 4 cm long and 2 cm wide.

4) Draw a rectangle whose length is 5 cm and whose width is 3 cm. What is the perimeter of the rectangle?

5) What is the perimeter of the rectangle?

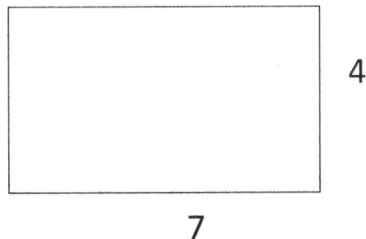

4

7

Perimeter: Find the Missing Side Lengths

✎Find the missing side of each shape.

1) perimeter = 88

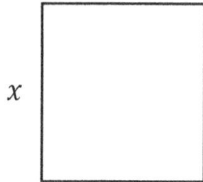

x

2) perimeter = 26

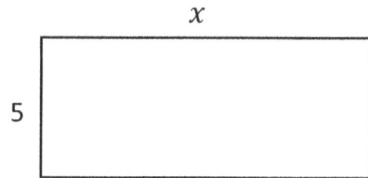

x

5

3) perimeter = 32

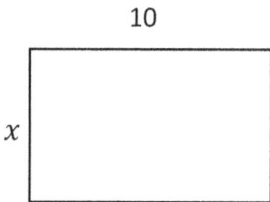

10

x

4) perimeter = 32

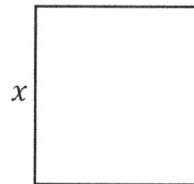

x

5) perimeter = 80

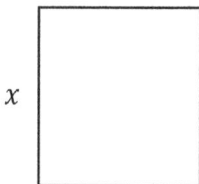

x

6) perimeter = 22

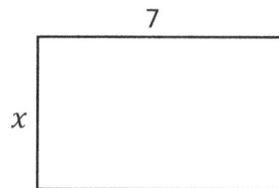

7

x

7) perimeter = 36

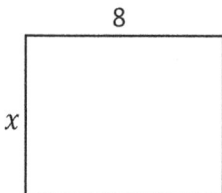

8

x

8) perimeter = 32

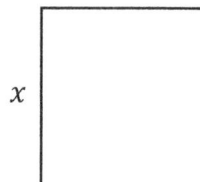

x

Perimeter and Area of Squares

✎Find perimeter and area of squares.

1) A: _____, P: _____

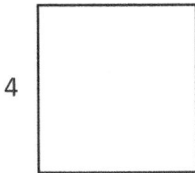

2) A: _____, P: _____

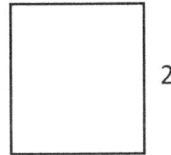

3) A: _____, P: _____

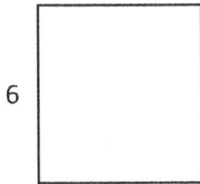

4) A: _____, P: _____

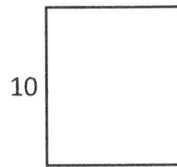

5) A: _____, P: _____

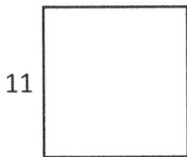

6) A: _____, P: _____

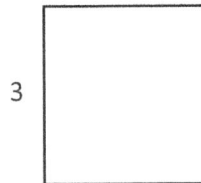

7) A: _____, P: _____

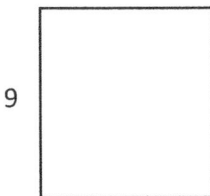

8) A: _____, P: _____

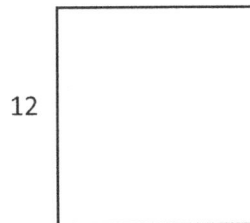

Perimeter and Area of rectangles

✎ *Find perimeter and area of rectangles.*

1) A: _____, P: _____

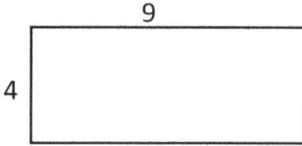

2) A: _____, P: _____

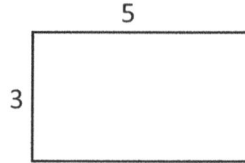

3) A: _____, P: _____

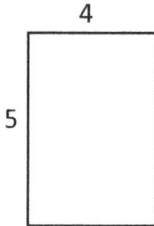

4) A: _____, P: _____

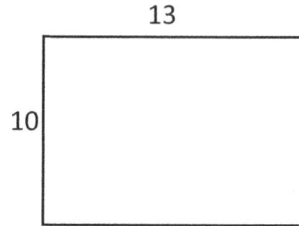

5) A: _____, P: _____

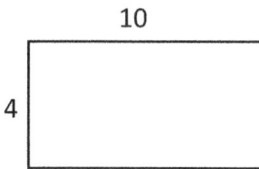

6) A: _____, P: _____

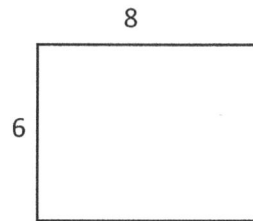

7) A: _____, P: _____

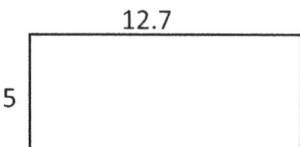

8) A: _____, P: _____

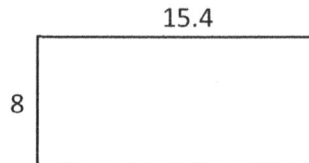

Find the Area or Missing Side Length of a Rectangle

Find area or missing side length of rectangles.

1) Area =?

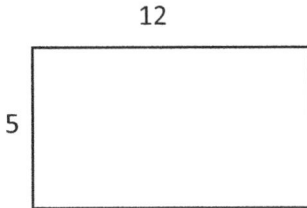

2) Area = 42, x =?

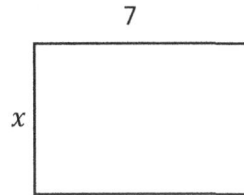

3) Area = 60, x =?

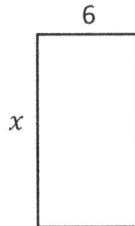

4) Area =?

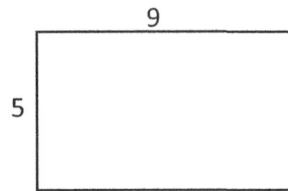

5) Area =?

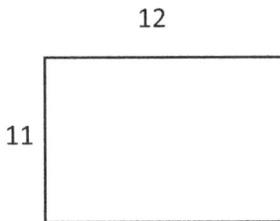

6) Area = 600, x =?

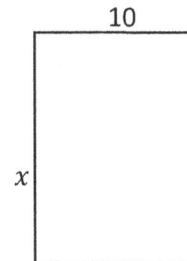

7) Area = 780, x =?

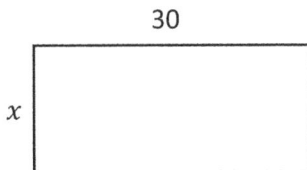

8) Area = 572, x =?

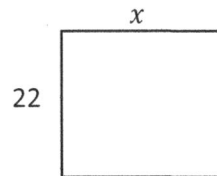

Area and Perimeter: Word Problems

✍*Solve.*

1) The area of a rectangle is 96 square meters. The width is 8 meters. What is the length of the rectangle?

2) A square has an area of 64 square feet. What is the perimeter of the square?

3) Ava built a rectangular vegetable garden that is 5 feet long and has an area of 45 square feet. What is the perimeter of Ava's vegetable garden?

4) A square has a perimeter of 96 millimeters. What is the area of the square?

5) The perimeter of David's square backyard is 88 meters. What is the area of David's backyard?

6) The area of a rectangle is 32 square inches. The length is 8 inches. What is the perimeter of the rectangle?

Volume of Cubes and Rectangle Prisms
Find the volume of each of the rectangular prisms.

1)

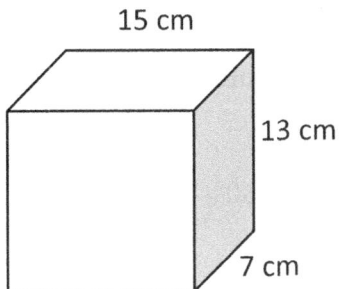

2)

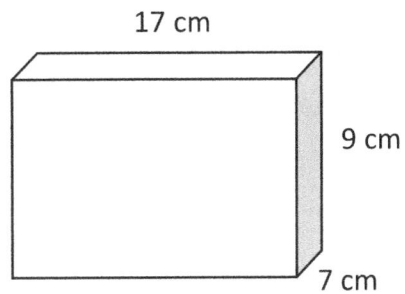

3)

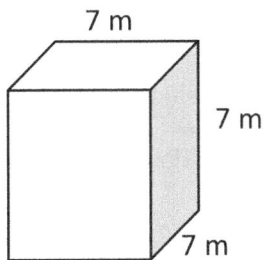

4)

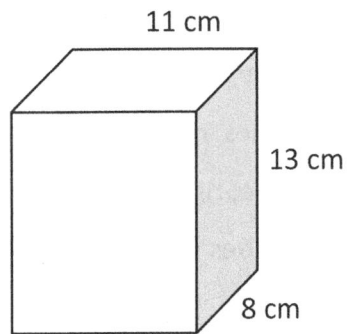

5)

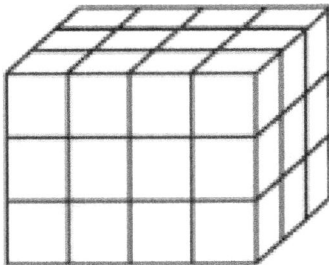

6)

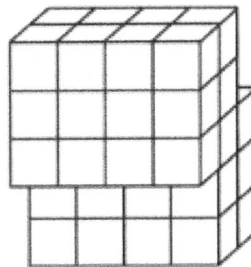

Answers of Worksheets – Chapter 8

Identifying Angles

1) Obtuse	3) Right	5) Straight	7) Obtuse
2) Acute	4) Acute	6) Obtuse	8) Acute

Estimate Angle Measurements

1) 90°	3) 110°	5) 130°	7) 25°
2) 180°	4) 60°	6) 75°	8) 95°

Polygon Names

1) Triangle	3) Pentagon	5) Heptagon
2) Quadrilateral	4) Hexagon	6) Octagon

Classify triangles

1) Scalene, obtuse	4) Equilateral, acute
2) Isosceles, right	5) Isosceles, acute
3) Scalene, right	6) Scalene, acute

Parallel Sides in Quadrilaterals

1) Square	3) Parallelogram	5) Trapezoid
2) Rectangle	4) Rhombus	6) Kike

Identify Rectangles

1) 4 - 4	3) Draw the rectangle	5) 22
2) 21	4) 16	

Perimeter: Find the Missing Side Lengths

1) 22	3) 6	5) 20	7) 10
2) 8	4) 8	6) 4	8) 8

Perimeter and Area of Squares

1) A: 16, P: 16	3) A: 36, P: 24	5) A: 121, P: 44
2) A: 4, P: 8	4) A: 100, P: 40	6) A: 9, P: 12

7) A: 81, P: 36   8) A: 144, P: 48

Perimeter and Area of rectangles

1) A: 36, P: 26	4) A: 130, P: 46	7) A: 63.5, P: 35.4
2) A: 15, P: 16	5) A: 40, P: 28	8) A: 123.2, P: 46.8
3) A: 20, P: 18	6) A: 48, P: 28	

Find the Area or Missing Side Length of a Rectangle

1) 60	4) 40	7) 26
2) 6	5) 132	8) 26
3) 10	6) 60	

Area and Perimeter: Word Problems

1) 12	3) 26	5) 484
2) 32	4) 576	6) 24

Volume of Cubes and Rectangle Prisms

1) 1,365 cm^3	4) 1,144 cm3
2) 1,071 cm3	5) 36
3) 343 m3	6) 44

Chapter 9: Three-Dimensional Figures

Topics that you'll learn in this chapter:

✓ Identify Three–Dimensional Figures

✓ Count Vertices, Edges, and Faces

✓ Identify Faces of Three–Dimensional Figures

Identify Three–Dimensional Figures

✎ *Write the name of each shape.*

1)

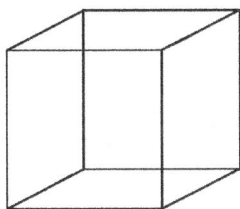

2)

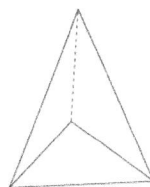

3)

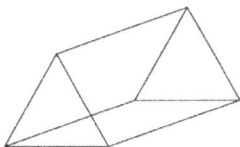

4)

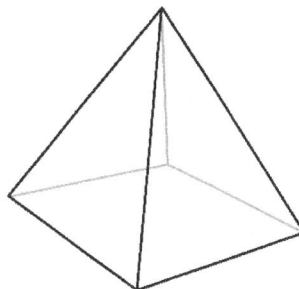

5)

6)

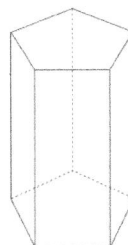

Count Vertices, Edges, and Faces

Shape	Number of edges	Number of faces	Number of vertices
1)	_____	_____	_____
2)	_____	_____	_____
3)	_____	_____	_____
4)	_____	_____	_____
5)	_____	_____	_____
6)	_____	_____	_____

Identify Faces of Three–Dimensional Figures

✎Write the number of faces.

1)

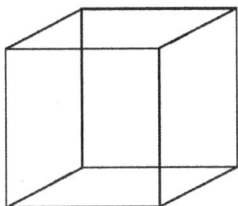

2)

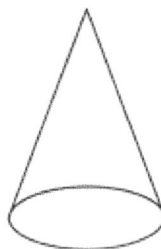

3)

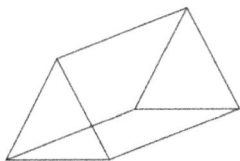

4)

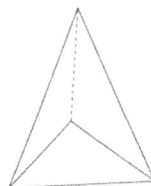

5)

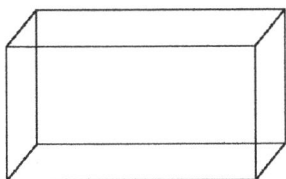

6)

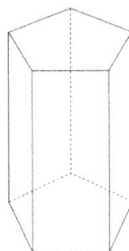

7)

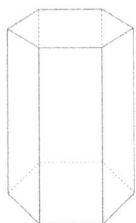

8)

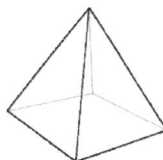

Answers of Worksheets – Chapter 9

Identify Three–Dimensional Figures

1) Cube

2) Triangular pyramid

3) Triangular prism

4) Square pyramid

5) Rectangular prism

6) Pentagonal prism

7) Hexagonal prism

Count Vertices, Edges, and Faces

Shape	Number of edges	Number of faces	Number of vertices
1)	6	4	4
2)	8	5	5
3)	12	6	8
4)	12	6	8
5)	15	7	10
6)	18	8	12

Identify Faces of Three–Dimensional Figures

1) 6	3) 5	5) 6	7) 8
2) 2	4) 4	6) 7	8) 5

Chapter 10: Symmetry and Transformations

Topics that you'll learn in this chapter:

- ✓ Line Segments
- ✓ Identify Lines of Symmetry
- ✓ Count Lines of Symmetry
- ✓ Parallel, Perpendicular and Intersecting Lines
- ✓ Translations, Rotations, and Reflections

Line Segments

Write each as a line, ray or line segment.

1)

2)

3)

4)

5)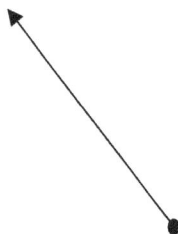

6)

7)

8)

Identify Lines of Symmetry

✍ Tell whether the line on each shape a line of symmetry is.

1)
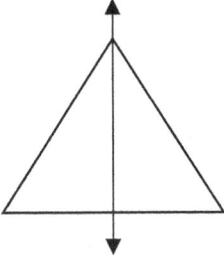

2)
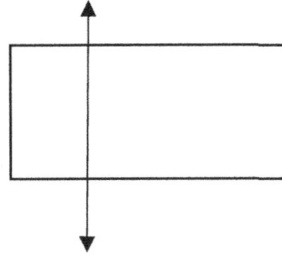

3)
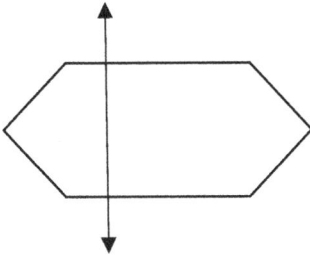

4)
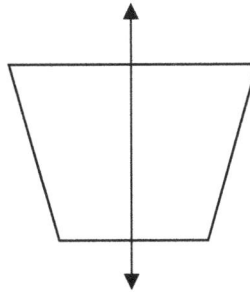

5)

6)
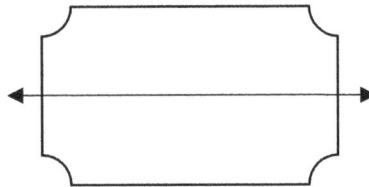

7)
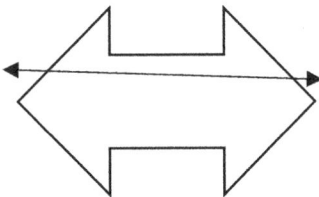

8)
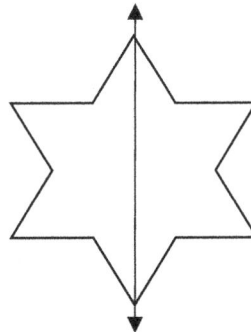

Count Lines of Symmetry

✎Draw lines of symmetry on each shape. Count and write the lines of symmetry you see.

1)

2)

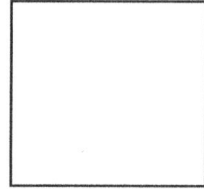

3)

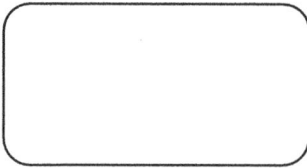

4)

5)

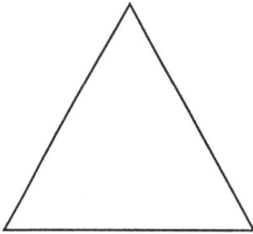

6)

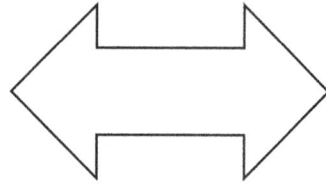

7)

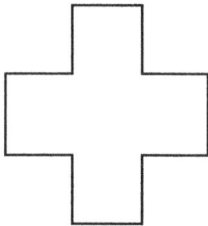

8)

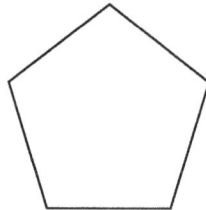

Parallel, Perpendicular and Intersecting Lines

✍ *State whether the given pair of lines are parallel,*

perpendicular, or intersecting.

1)

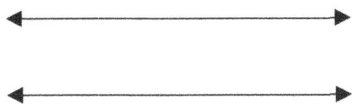

2)

3)

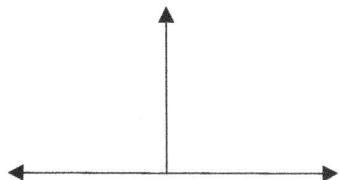

4)

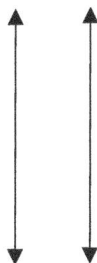

5)

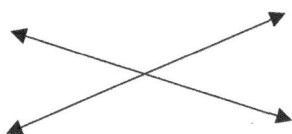

6)

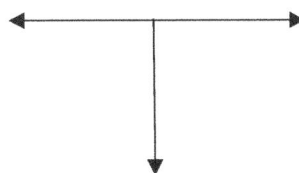

7)

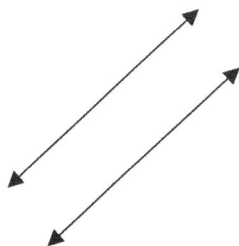

8)

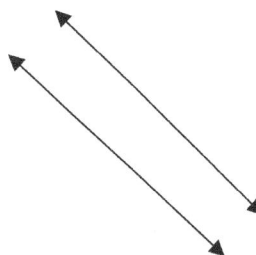

Answers of Worksheets – Chapter 10

Line Segments

1) Line segment
2) Ray
3) Line

4) Line segment
5) Ray
6) Line

7) Line
8) Line segment

Identify lines of symmetry

1) yes
2) no

3) no
4) yes

5) yes
6) yes

7) no
8) yes

Count lines of symmetry

1)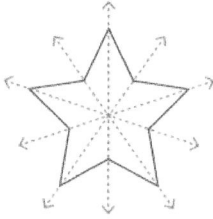

2)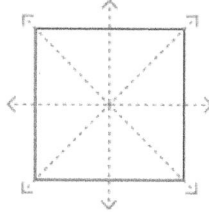

3)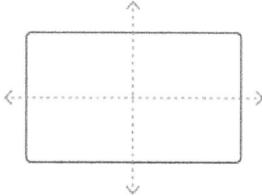

4)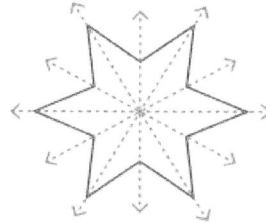

5)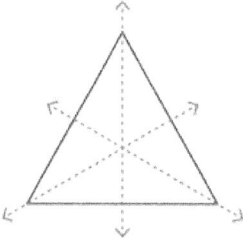

6)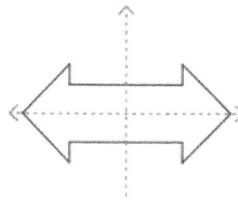

7)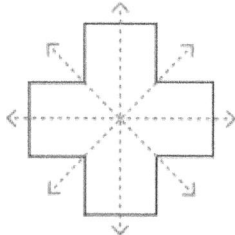

8)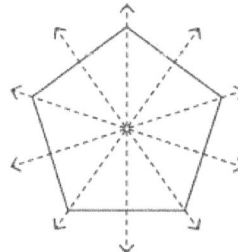

Parallel, Perpendicular and Intersecting Lines

1) Parallel
2) Intersection
3) Perpendicular
4) Parallel

5) Intersection
6) Perpendicular
7) Parallel
8) Parallel

Chapter 11: Data and Graphs

Topics that you'll learn in this chapter:

✓ Graph Points on a Coordinate Plane

✓ Bar Graph

✓ Tally and Pictographs

✓ Line Graphs

✓ Stem–And–Leaf Plot

✓ Scatter Plots

Graph Points on a Coordinate Plane

✎ *Plot each point on the coordinate grid.*

1) A (4, 6)   3) C (3, 7)   5) E (6, 5)

2) B (1, 5)   4) D (8, 3)   6) F (9, 7)

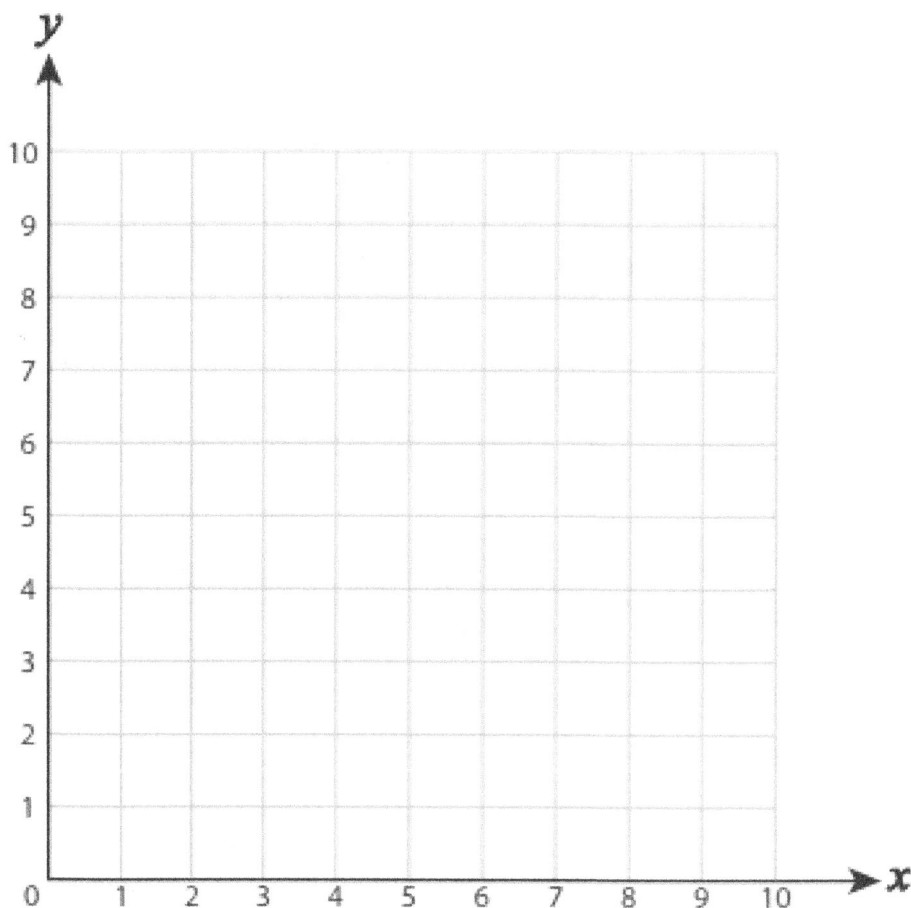

Bar Graph

Graph the given information as a bar graph.

Day	Hot dogs sold
Monday	50
Tuesday	70
Wednesday	30
Thursday	90
Friday	80

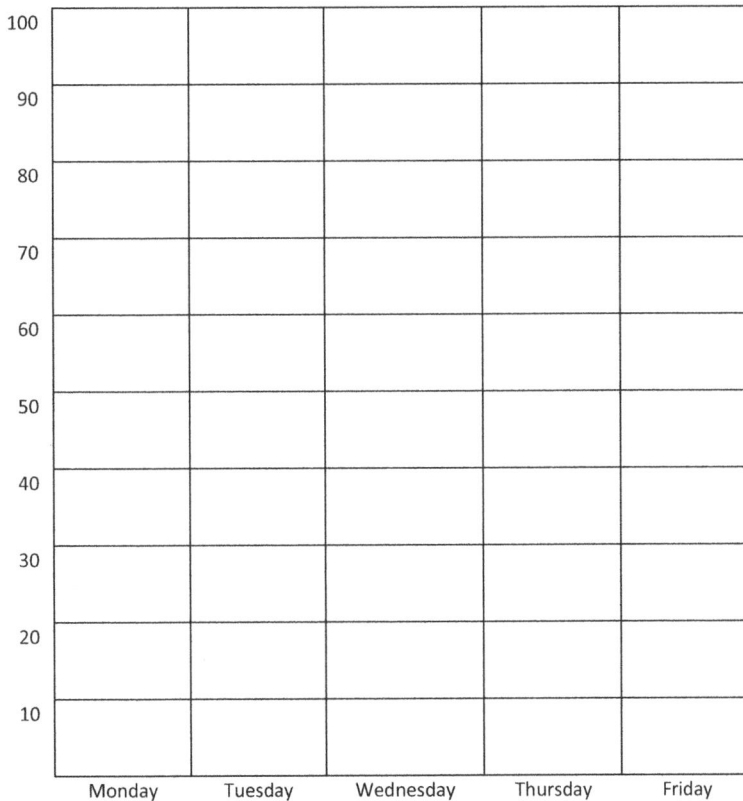

	Monday	Tuesday	Wednesday	Thursday	Friday
100					
90					
80					
70					
60					
50					
40					
30					
20					
10					

Tally and Pictographs

Using the key, draw the pictograph to show the information.

🐑	IIII
🦨	IIII I
🦋	IIII III
🐟	II
🐸	IIII IIII II

🐑	
🦨	
🦋	
🐟	
🐸	

Key: 🙂 = 2 animals

Line Graphs

David work as a salesman in a store. He records the number of shoes sold in five days on a line graph. Use the graph to answer the question

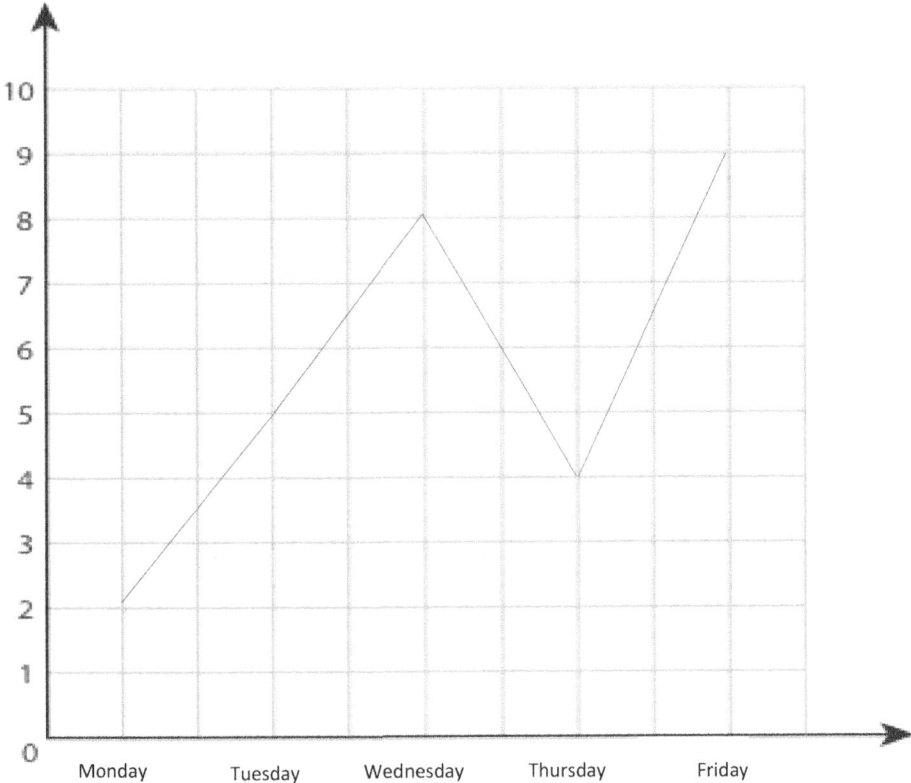

1) How many shoes were sold on Tuesday?

2) Which day had the minimum sales of shoes?

3) Which day had the maximum number of shoes sold?

4) How many shoes were sold in 5 days?

Stem–And–Leaf Plot

Make stem ad leaf plots for the given data.

1) 22, 24, 27, 21, 52, 24, 58, 57, 29, 24, 19, 12

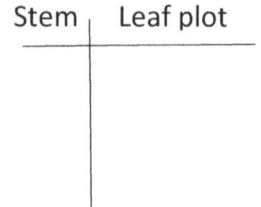

Stem	Leaf plot

2) 11, 45, 34, 18, 15, 11, 32, 41, 40, 30, 45, 35

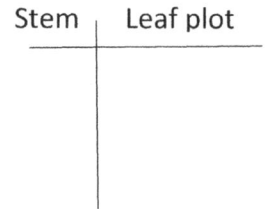

Stem	Leaf plot

3) 112, 87, 96, 85, 100, 117, 92, 114, 88, 112, 98, 107

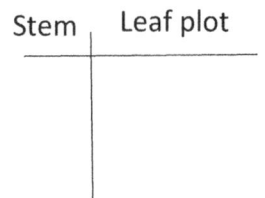

Stem	Leaf plot

4) 63, 50, 104, 63, 72, 56, 109 63, 75, 59, 63, 108, 79

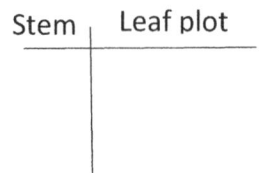

Stem	Leaf plot

Scatter Plots

✍ *Construct a scatter plot.*

x	1	2	3	4	5	8
y	15	25	40	60	75	50

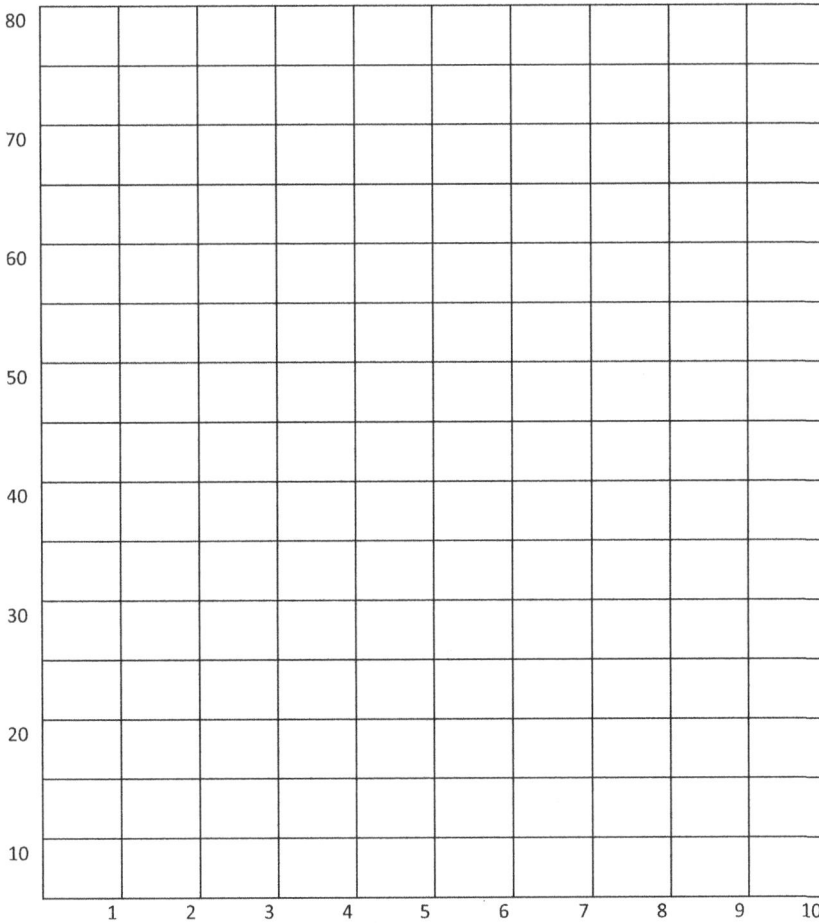

Answers of Worksheets – Chapter 11

Graph Points on a Coordinate Plane

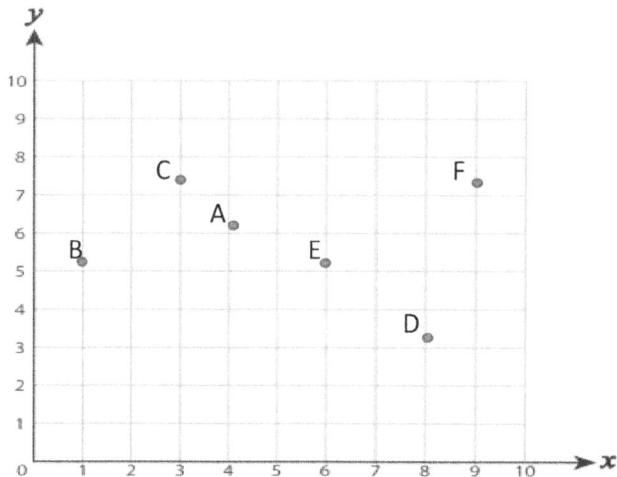

Bar Graph

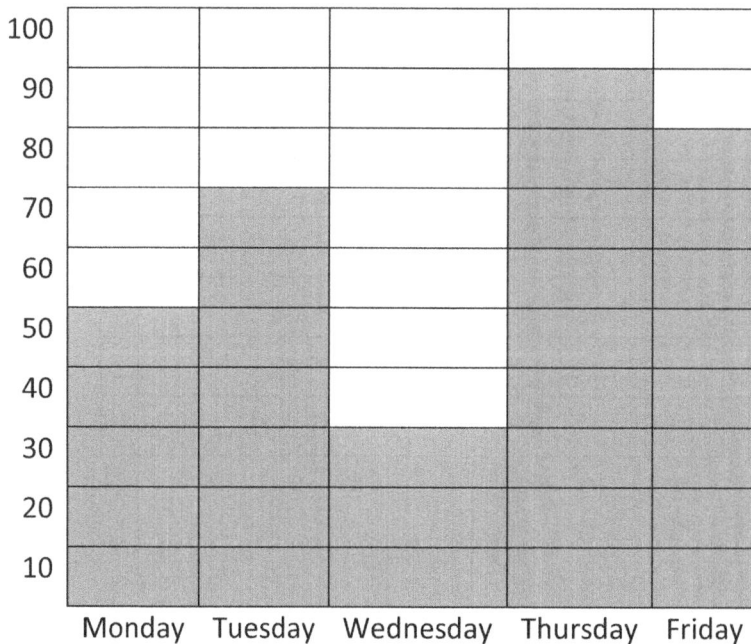

Tally and Pictographs

Line *Graphs*

1) 5   2) Monday   3) Friday   4) 28

Stem–And–Leaf Plot

1)	Stem	leaf
	1	2 9
	2	1 2 4 4 4 7 9
	5	2 7 8

2)	Stem	leaf
	1	1 1 5 8
	3	0 2 4 5
	4	0 1 5 5

3)	Stem	leaf
	8	5 7 8
	9	2 6 8
	10	0 7
	11	2 2 4 7

4)	Stem	leaf
	5	0 6 9
	6	3 3 3 3
	7	2 5 9
	10	4 8 9

Scatter Plots

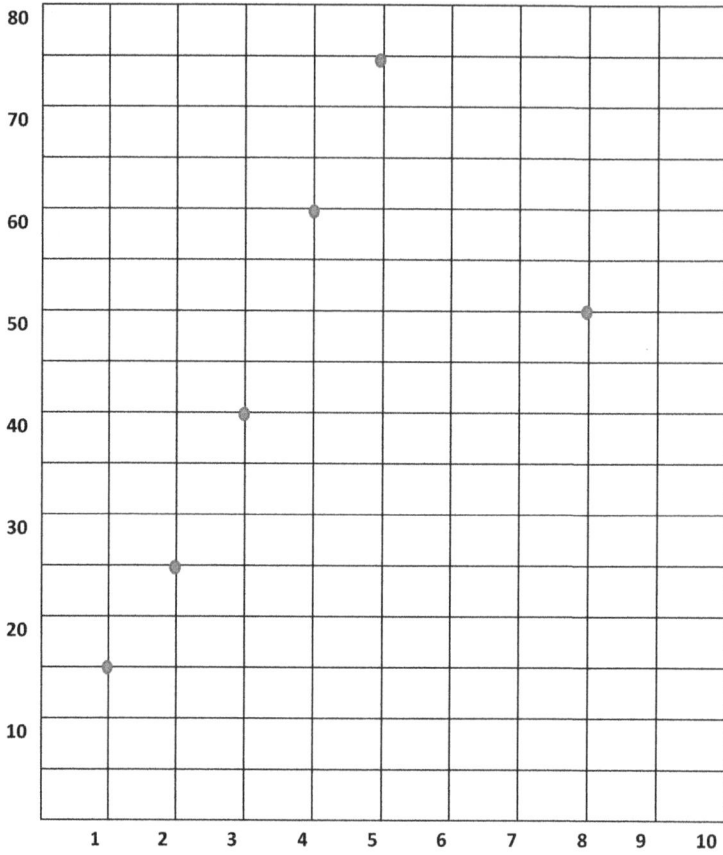

SBAC Math Practice Tests

Smarter Balanced Assessment Consortium (SBAC) test assesses student mastery of the common core State Standards.

The SBAC is a computer adaptive test. It means that there is a set of test questions in a variety of question types that adjust to each student based on the student's answers to previous questions. This section includes a range of items types, such as selecting several correct responses for one item, typing out a response, fill---in short answers/tables, graphing, drag and drop, etc.

On computer adaptive tests, if the correct answer is chosen, the next question will be harder. If the answer given is incorrect, the next question will be easier. This also means that once an answer is selected on the computer it cannot be changed.

In this section, there are 2 complete SBAC Math Tests that reflect the format and question types on SBAC. On a real SBAC Math test, the number of questions varies and there are about 30 questions.

Let your student take these tests to see what score he or she will be able to receive on a real SBAC test.

Time to Test

Time to refine your skill with a practice examination

Take a REAL SBAC Mathematics test to simulate the test day experience. After you've finished, score your test using the answer key.

Before You Start

- You'll need a pencil and scratch papers to take the test.
- For this practice test, don't time yourself. Spend time as much as you need.
- It's okay to guess. You won't lose any points if you're wrong.
- After you've finished the test, review the answer key to see where you went wrong.

Calculators are not permitted for SBAC Tests

Good Luck!

SBAC GRADE 4 MAHEMATICS REFRENCE MATERIALS

Conversions:

LENGTH

Customary	Metric
1 mile (mi) = 1,760 yards (yd)	1 kilometer (km) = 1,000 meters (m)
1 yard (yd) = 3 feet (ft)	1 meter (m) = 100 centimeters (cm)
1 foot (ft) = 12 inches (in.)	1 centimeter (cm) = 10 millimeters (mm)

VOLUME AND CAPACITY

Customary	Metric
1 gallon (gal) = 4 quarts (qt)	1 liter (L) = 1,000 milliliters (mL)
1 quart (qt) = 2 pints (pt.)	
1 pint (pt.) = 2 cups (c)	
1 cup (c) = 8 fluid ounces (Fl oz)	

WEIGHT AND MASS

Customary	Metric
1 ton (T) = 2,000 pounds (lb.)	1 kilogram (kg) = 1,000 grams (g)
1 pound (lb.) = 16 ounces (oz)	1 gram (g) = 1,000 milligrams (mg)

Time

1 year = 12 months	1 day = 24 hours
1 year = 52 weeks	1 hour = 60 minutes
1 week = 7 days	1 minute = 60 seconds

Formulas:

Perimeter

Square	$P = 4S$
Rectangle	$P = L + W + L + W$ or $P = 2L + 2W$

Area

Square	$A = S \times S$
Rectangle	$A = L \times W$

Smarter Balanced Assessment Consortium

SBAC Practice Test 1

Mathematics

GRADE 4

- ❖ **30 questions**
- ❖ **There is no time limit for this practice test.**
- ❖ **Calculators are NOT permitted for this practice test**

Administered Month Year

1) Which statement about the number 574,382.16 is true?

   A. The digit 7 has a value of (7 × 1000)

   B. The digit 4 has a value of (4 × 100)

   C. The digit 8 has a value of (8 × 10)

   D. The digit 5 has a value of (5 × 100)

2) What is the perimeter of this rectangle?

   A. 12 cm

   B. 24 cm

   C. 32 cm

   D. 18 cm

   6 cm

   3 cm

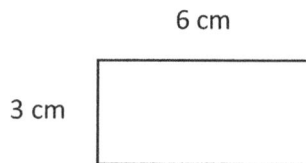

3) What is the eighth number in the following pattern?

   1,250, 1,400, 1,1550, 1,700, _____, _____, _____, _____

   A. 1,830

   B. 1,950

   C. 2,070

   D. 2,300

4) Jamie has 5 quarters, 8 dime, and 11 pennies. How much money does Jamie have?

   A. 150 pennies

   B. 240 pennies

   C. 216 pennies

   D. 281 pennies

5) Jeb paid $84 for a magazine subscription. If he is paying $4 for each issue of the magazine, how many issues of the magazine will he receive?

   A. 18

   B. 21

   C. 22

   D. 24

6) What is the perimeter of the triangle?

   A. 27 inches

   B. 31 inches

   C. 39 inches

   D. 152 inches

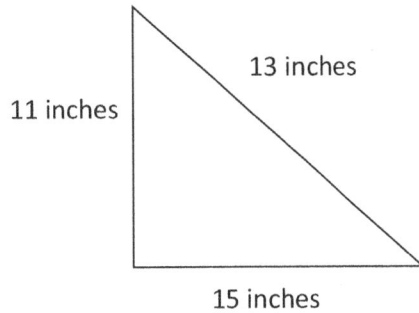

13 inches

11 inches

15 inches

7) Emma draws a shape on her paper. The shape has four sides. It has only one pair of parallel sides. What shape does Emma draw?

   A. parallelogram

   B. rectangle

   C. square

   D. trapezoid

8) Order the fractions from least to greatest. $\frac{3}{4}, \frac{2}{3}, \frac{5}{6}, \frac{1}{2}$

A. $\frac{3}{4}, \frac{5}{6}, \frac{2}{3}, \frac{1}{2}$

B. $\frac{5}{6}, \frac{3}{4}, \frac{1}{2}, \frac{2}{3}$

C. $\frac{1}{2}, \frac{2}{3}, \frac{3}{4}, \frac{5}{6}$

D. $\frac{2}{3}, \frac{1}{2}, \frac{5}{6}, \frac{3}{4}$

9) There were 23 students in the first row and 7 students in the second row. How many students were in the first two rows?

A. 30

B. 34

C. 77

D. 86

10) The figure below shows a diagram of a living room.

The perimeter of the living room is 40 feet (ft). What is the width(w) of the living room?

A. 10 ft

B. 15 ft

C. 20 ft

D. 30 ft

Living Room

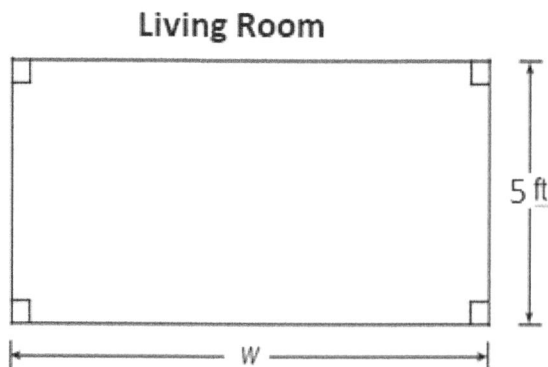

5 ft

w

11) Jack has $54.70. He earns $13.90 more. How much money does Jack have in all?

    A. $183.70

    B. $40.80

    C. $67.60

    D. $68.60

12) Joe put 14 red cards and 5 black cards in each bag. What is the total number of cards Joe put in 7 bags?

    A. 133

    B. 98

    C. 35

    D. 26

13) A football teams play 82 games each year. How many games will the team play in 13 years?

    A. 1,080

    B. 1,140

    C. 1,066

    D. 1,680

14) Which number is represented by A? $8 \times A = 120$

    A. 15

    B. 10

    C. 11

    D. 12

15) A building is 27 feet high. What is the height of the building in yards?

    A. 1 yard

    B. 9 yards

    C. 15 yards

    D. 109 yards

16) The sum of A and B equals 37. If A = 12, which equation can be used to find the value of B?

    A. B – 12 = 37

    B. B + 12 = 37

    C. A + 12 = 37

    D. A – 12 = 37

17) Which triangle has one obtuse angle?

A.
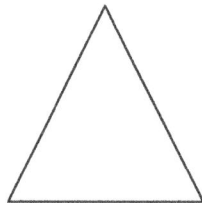

C.
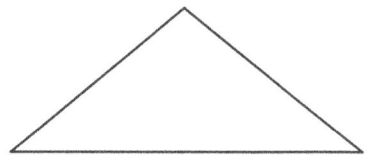

B
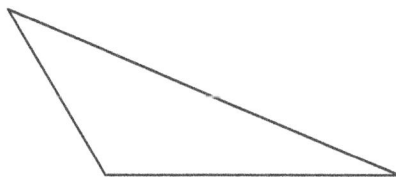

D.
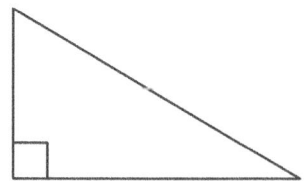

18) Lisa has 210 pastilles. She wants to put them in boxes of 15 pastilles. How many boxes does she need?

    A. 16

    B. 12

    C. 18

    D. 14

19) What is the volume of the cube?

    A. 15

    B. 60

    C. 125

    D. 600

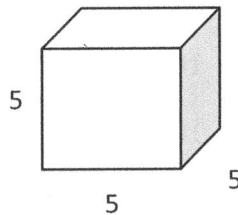

20) To what number is the arrow pointing?

    A. 14

    B. 16

    C. 18

    D. 20

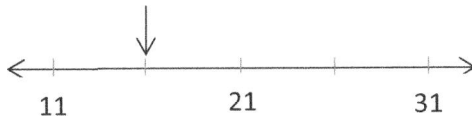

21) What mixed number is shown by the shaded rectangles?

    A. $3\frac{1}{4}$

    B. $3\frac{3}{4}$

    C. $2\frac{1}{4}$

    D. $2\frac{3}{4}$

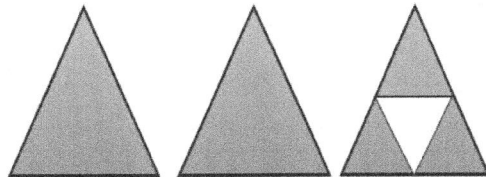

22) A straight-line measure 180°. A straight line and a triangle are touching as shown in the figure below.

What is the value of *A* in the figure?

A. 64

B. 84

C. 90

D. 96

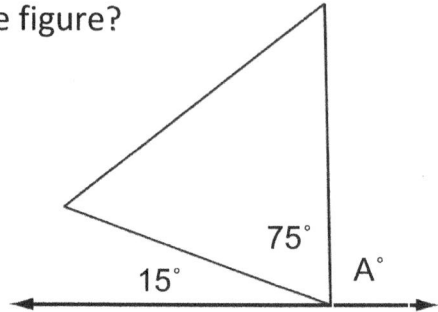

23) The number 42.06 can be expressed as _____

A. $(4 \times 10) + (2 \times 1) + (6 \times 0.01)$

B. $(4 \times 10) + (2 \times 1) + (6 \times 0.1)$

C. $(4 \times 1) + (2 \times 1) + (0 \times 1) + (6 \times 1)$

D. $(4 \times 10) + (2 \times 1) + (0 \times 10) + (6 \times 100)$

24) What is the perimeter of this shape?

A. 14

B. 48

C. 18

D. 16

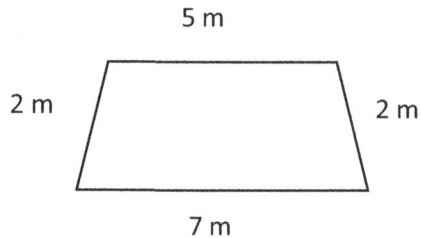

25) Which fraction has the least value?

A. $\frac{1}{4}$

B. $\frac{3}{8}$

C. $\frac{12}{16}$

D. $\frac{11}{16}$

26) The temperature on Sunday at 12:00 PM was 74°F. Low temperature on the same day was 34°F cooler. Which temperature is closest to the low temperature on that day?

A. 76°F

B. 40°F

C. 51°F

D. 75°

27) Which shape shows a line of symmetry?

A.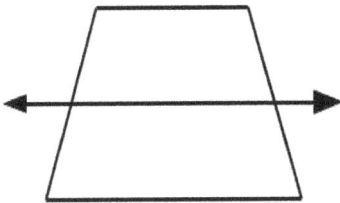

C.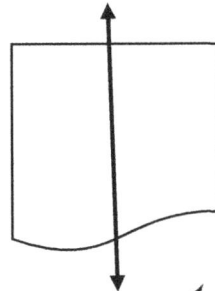

B.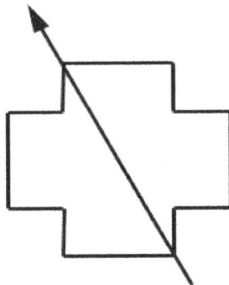

D.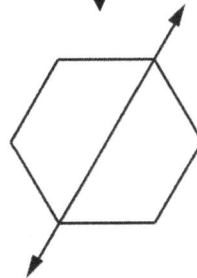

28) There are 365 days in a year, and 24 hours in a day. How many hours are in a year?

A. 7440

B. 6250

C. 8563

D. 8760

29) On Sunday Leon was a referee at 3 soccer games. He arrived at the soccer field 25 minutes before the first game. Each game lasted for 45 minutes. There were 15 minutes between each game. Leon left 15 minutes after the last game. How long, in minutes, was Leon at the soccer field?

    A. 220 minutes

    B. 205 minutes

    C. 190 minutes

    D. 180 minutes

30) Rounded to the nearest 10,000, the population of Louisiana was 56,820,000 in 2010. Which number could be the actual population of Louisiana in 2010?

    A. 56,719,496

    B. 56,826,184

    C. 56,824,720

    D. 56,830,148

"This is the end of Practice Test 1"

Smarter Balanced Assessment Consortium

SBAC Practice Test 2

Mathematics

GRADE 4

❖ **30 questions**

❖ **There is no time limit for this practice test.**

❖ **Calculators are NOT permitted for this practice test**

Administered *Month Year*

1) Use a rule to measure the length and width of the following rectangle to the nearest inches.

   What measurement is the closest to the area of the rectangle in square inches?

   A. 12 square inches

   B. 16 square inches

   C. 9 square inches

   D. 14 square inches

2) There are 7 days in a week. There are 42 days in the month of February. How many times as many days are there in February than are in one week?

   A. 5 times

   B. 4 times

   C. 6 times

   D. 30 times

3) A football team is buying new uniforms. Each uniform costs $35. The team wants to buy 12 uniforms.

Which equation represents a way to find the total cost of the uniforms?

A. $(30 \times 10) + (5 \times 5) = 300 + 25$

B. $(30 \times 5) + (10 \times 5) = 150 + 50$

C. $(35 \times 10) + (35 \times 2) = 350 + 70$

D. $(35 \times 5) + (5 \times 12) = 175 + 60$

4) A number sentence such as $18 + Z = 86$ can be called an equation. If this equation is true, then which of the following equations is not true?

A. $86 - 18 = Z$

B. $86 - Z = 18$

C. $Z - 18 = 86$

D. $Z + 18 = 86$

5) Ella described a number using these clues:

Three – digit odd numbers that have a 7 in the hundreds place and a 5 in the tens place. Which number could fit Ella's description?

A. 758

B. 757

C. 752

D. 756

6) Which number correctly completes the number sentence 70 ×

42 =?

   A. 2,940

   B. 870

   C. 1,820

   D. 2,920

7) Tam has 360 cards. He wants to put them in boxes of 40cards.

   How many boxes does he need?

   A. 7

   B. 9

   C. 11

   D. 13

8) If this clock shows a time in the morning, what time was it 4

   hours and 30 minutes ago?

   A. 07:45 AM

   B. 09:45 AM

   C. 09:45 PM

   D. 07:45 PM

9) Joe has 3,754 crayons. What is this number rounded to the

   nearest hundred?

   A. 3,750

   B. 3,760

   C. 3,700

   D. 3,800

10) Use the table below to answer the question.

Favorite Sports

Sport	Number of Votes
football (FB)	10
basketball (BB)	5
soccer (SOC)	7
volleyball (VB)	3

The students in the fourth-grade class voted for their favorite sport. Which bar graph shows results of the students vote?

A.

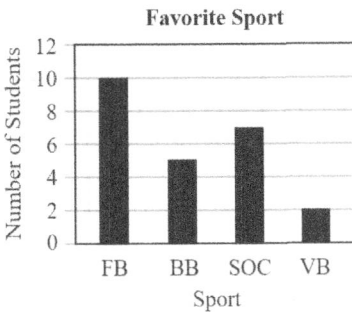

B.

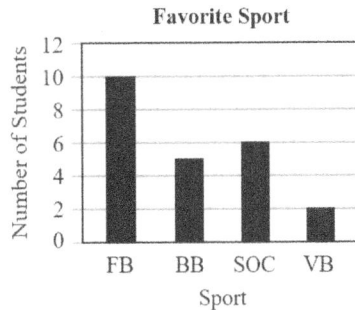

C.

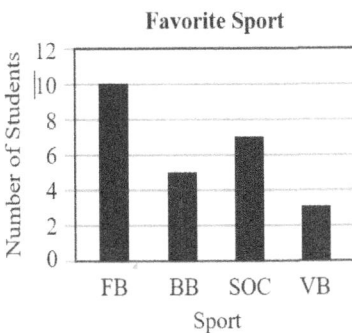

D.

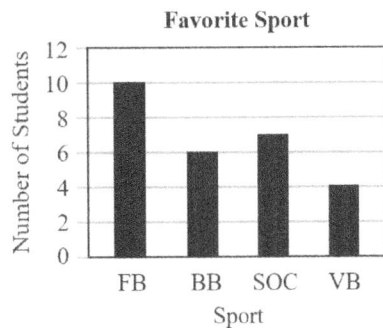

11) Use the picture below to answer the question.

Which decimal number names the shaded part of this square?

A. 0.08

B. 0.20

C. 0.92

D. 0.89

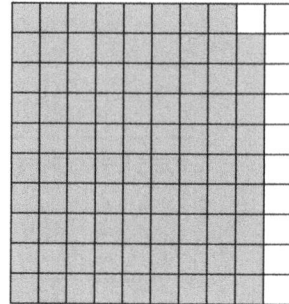

12) Use the table below to answer the question.

Which list of city populations is in order from least to greatest?

A. 28,751; 23,086; 29,980; 26,370.

B. 23,086; 26,370; 28,751; 29,980.

C. 26,370; 28,751; 29,980;23,086.

D. 29,980; 28,751; 26,370; 23,086.

City Populations	
City	Population
Denton	23,086
Bomberg	26,307
Windham	28,751
Sanhill	29,980

13) Which number correctly completes the subtraction sentence

$6.0 - 4.15 = $ _____ ?

A. 1.45

B. 1.85

C. 2.25

D. 3.65

14) For a concert, there are children's tickets and adult tickets for sale. Of the total available tickets, $\frac{46}{100}$ have been sold as adult tickets and $\frac{3}{10}$ as children's tickets. The rest of the tickets have not been sold.

What fraction of the total number of tickets for the concert have been sold?

A. $1\frac{24}{76}$

B. $\frac{19}{25}$

C. $\frac{100}{76}$

D. $\frac{77}{120}$

15) Circle a reasonable measurement for the angle F:

A. 45°

B. 90°

C. 180°

D. 240°

F

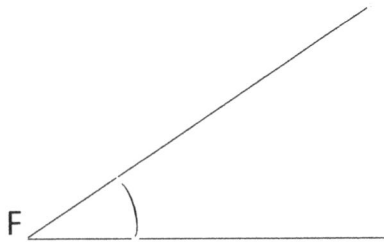

16) Peter's pencil is $\frac{15}{100}$ of a meter long. What is the length, in meters, of Peter's pencil written as a decimal?

A. 0.15

B. 1.05

C. 1.5

D. 15.100

17) Mia has a group of shapes. Each shape in her group has at least one set of parallel sides. Each shape also has at least one set of perpendicular sides. Which group could be Mia's group of shapes?

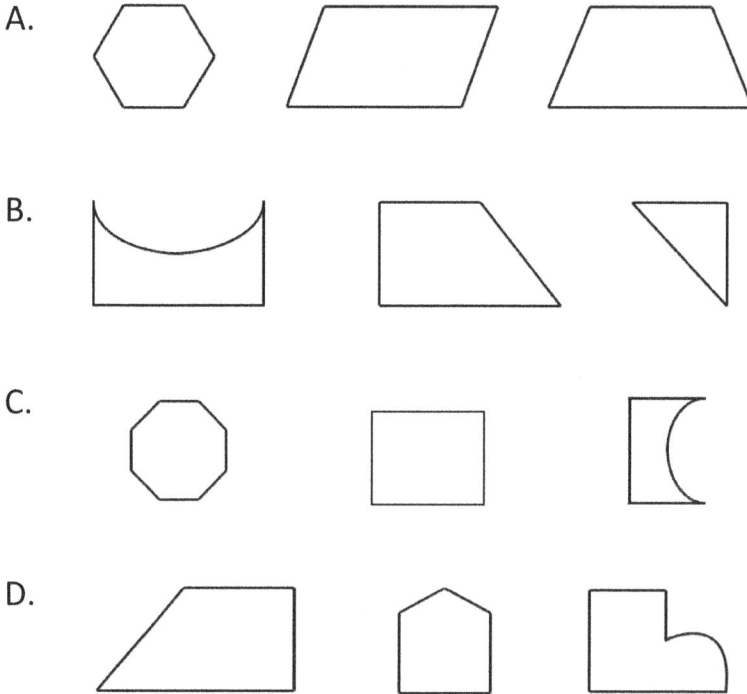

A.

B.

C.

D.

18) There are 75 students from Riddle Elementary school at the library on Monday. The other 52 students in the school are practicing in the classroom. Which number sentence shows the total number of students in Riddle Elementary school?

A. 75 + 52

B. 75 − 52

C. 75 × 52

D. 75 ÷ 52

19) A stack of 5 pennies has a height of 1 centimeter. Elise has a stack of pennies with a height of 7 centimeters. Which equation can be used to find the number of pennies, n, in Elise's stack of pennies?

A. $n = 7 + 5$

B. $n = 7 - 5$

C. $n = 5 \times 7$

D. $n = 7 \div 5$

20) Use the models below to answer the question.

Which statement about the models is true?

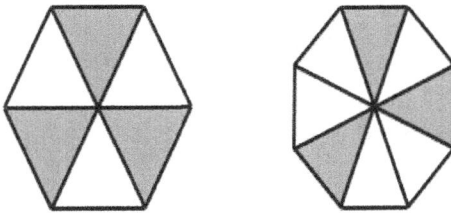

A. Each shows the same fraction because they are the same size.

B. Each shows a different fraction because they are different shapes.

C. Each shows the same fraction because they both have 3 sections shaded.

D. Each shows a different fraction because they both have 3 shaded sections but a different number of total sections.

21) What is the value of A in the equation $81 \div A = 9$?

   A. 3

   B. 9

   C. 7

   D. 8

22) Sophia flew 5, 338 miles from Los Angeles to New York City. What is the number of miles Sophia flew rounded to the nearest thousand?

   A. 5,000

   B. 5,300

   C. 5,400

   D. 6,000

23) Write $\frac{325}{1000}$ as a decimal number.

   A. 3.25

   B. 0.325

   C. 32.5

   D. 0.0325

24) Erik made 15 pints of juice. He drinks 5 cups of juice each day. How many days will Erik take to drink all of the juice he made?

   A. 2 days

   B. 3 days

   C. 7 days

   D. 6 days

25) Jason has prepared $\frac{8}{10}$ of his assignment. Which decimal represent the part of the assignment Jason has prepared?

   A. 8.10

   B. 8.01

   C. 0.8

   D. 0.08

26) Emma described a number using these clues.

   ✓ 3 digits of the number are 4, 7, and 9

   ✓ The value of the digit 4 is (4 × 10)

   ✓ The value of the digit 7 is (7 × 1000)

   ✓ The value of the digit 9 is (9 × 10000)

   Which number could fit Emma's description?

   A. 9,724.04

   B. 90,734.40

   C. 97,045.04

   D. 98,740.70

27) There are 17 boxes and each box contain 23 pencils. How many pencils are in the boxed in total?

   A. 108

   B. 280

   C. 391

   D. Not here

28) Emily and Ava were working on a group project last week. They completed $\frac{8}{10}$ of their project on Tuesday and the rest on Wednesday.

Ava completed $\frac{7}{10}$ of their project on Tuesday. What fraction of the group project did Emily completed on Tuesday?

A. $\frac{2}{10}$

B. $\frac{3}{10}$

C. $\frac{1}{10}$

D. $\frac{7}{10}$

29) Moe packs 66 boxes with flashcards. Each box holds 100 flashcards. How many flashcards Moe can pack into these boxes?

A. 6600

B. 660

C. 275

D. 6,650

30) Jason's favorite sports team has won 0.76 of its games this season. How can Jason express this decimal as a fraction?

A. $\frac{6}{2}$

B. $\frac{76}{10}$

C. $\frac{76}{100}$

D. $\frac{7.6}{10}$

"This is the end of Practice Test 2"

Answers and Explanations

SBAC Practice Tests

Answer Key

❋ Now, it's time to review your results to see where you went wrong and what areas you need to improve!

SBAC - Mathematics

Practice Test - 1						Practice Test - 2					
1	C	11	D	21	D	1	A	11	D	21	B
2	D	12	A	22	C	2	C	12	B	22	A
3	D	13	C	23	A	3	C	13	B	23	B
4	C	14	A	24	D	4	C	14	B	24	B
5	A	15	B	25	A	5	B	15	A	25	C
6	C	16	B	26	B	6	D	16	A	26	C
7	D	17	B	27	D	7	B	17	D	27	C
8	C	18	D	28	D	8	C	18	A	28	C
9	A	19	C	29	B	9	D	19	C	29	A
10	B	20	B	30	C	10	C	20	D	30	C

Practice Test 1

SBAC - Mathematics

Answers and Explanations

1) Answer: C.

A. The digit 7 has a value of $7 \times 1/1000$, not 7×1000.

B. The digit 4 has a value of $4 \times 10,000$, not 4×100.

C. The digit 8 has a value of 8×10. This is true!

D. The digit 5 has a value of $5 \times 1,000$, not 5×100.

2) Answer: D.

use perimeter of rectangle formula.

P = 2 (length + width)

$P = 2 \times (3 + 6) = 2 \times 9 = 18$ cm

3) Answer: D.

The difference of each two successive numbers is 150.

Add four 150 to last number (1,700): $1,700 + 150 + 150 + 150 + 150$

$= 2,300$

4) Answer: C.

5 quarters = 5×25 pennies = 125 pennies

8 dimes = 8×10 pennies = 80 pennies

In total Nicole has 216 pennies

5) Answer: A.

1 issue of the magazine = $4

$84 ÷ $4 = 21 issues of the magazine

6) Answer: C.

To find the perimeter of a triangle, add all three sides of the triangle.

P = 11 + 15 + 13 = 39 inches

7) Answer: D.

A quadrilateral with one pair of parallel sides is a trapezoid.

8) Answer: C.

To compare fractions, we can write fractions with the same denominator. Then, we can compare the numerators of each fraction and put them in correct order from least to greatest or greatest to least.

Common denominator of 4, 3, 6 and 2 is 12. Rewrite the fractions:

$$\frac{3}{4} = \frac{9}{12} \qquad \frac{2}{3} = \frac{8}{12} \qquad \frac{5}{6} = \frac{10}{12} \qquad \frac{1}{2} = \frac{6}{12}$$

9) Answer: A.

$23 + 7 = 30$

10) Answer: B.

Use perimeter of rectangle formula.

P = 2 × (Length + Width)

40 = 2 × (5 + W) ⇒ 40 = 10 + 2 × W

⇒ 2 × W = 40 − 10 = 30 ⇒ W = 15 feet

11) Answer: D.

$54.70 + $13.90 = $68.60

12) Answer: A.

1 bag = 14 red cards + 5 black cards (14 + 5 = 19 cards)

7 bags = 7 × 19 = 133 cards

13)Answer: C.

1 year = 82 games

13 years = 13 × 82 = 1,066 games

14)Answer: A.

A = 120 ÷ 8 = 15

15)Answer: B.

3 feet = 1 yard;   27 feet = 9 yards

16)Answer: B.

The sum of A and B equals 35: A + B = 37, if A = 12,

then B = 37 − 12 = 25.   12 + 25 = 37 or B + 12 = 37

17)Answer: B.

An obtuse triangle is one with one obtuse angle (greater than 90°)

and two acute angles. Since a triangle's angles must add up to 180°,

no triangle can have more than one obtuse angle.

Only shape B has one obtuse angle.

18)Answer: D.

15 pastilles = 1 box

210 pastilles = (210 ÷ 15) = 14 boxes

19)Answer: C.

To find the volume of cube, multiply one side of the cube by itself 3

times:

Volume of a cube = (side) × (side) × (side) = 5 × 5 × 5 = 125

20) Answer: B.

Arrow is pointing to a number in the middle of two numbers 11 and 21. Therefore, the answer is 16.

21) Answer: D.

This shape shows 2 complete shaded triangle and a three of a four part of triangle. The mixed number for this shape is $2\frac{3}{4}$.

22) Answer: C.

Three angles in a triangle add up to 180°.

A° + 75° + 15° = 180° ⇒ A° = 180° − 90° = 90°

23) Answer: A.

The number 42.06 can be expressed as:

(4 × 10) + (2 × 1) + (6 × 0.01) = 40 + 2 + 0.06 = 42.06

24) Answer: D.

To find the perimeter of the shape, add all four sides.

P = 2 + 7 + 2 + 5 = 16

25) Answer: A.

To compare fractions, we can write fractions with the same denominator. Then, we can compare the numerators of each fraction and put them in correct order from least to greatest or greatest to least.

Common denominator of 2, 8, 4 and 16 is 16. Rewrite the fractions:

A. $\frac{1}{4} = \frac{4}{16}$ B. $\frac{3}{8} = \frac{6}{16}$ C. $\frac{12}{16}$ B. $\frac{9}{16}$

26) Answer: B.

Low temperature is 24°f cooler than the temperature at 12:00 PM which is 76°. Low temperature is 40°f (74°f − 34°f) that is choice B.

27)Answer: D.

You can find if a shape has a Line of Symmetry by folding it. When the folded part sits perfectly on top (all edges matching), then the fold line is a Line of Symmetry. Shape D shows a line of symmetry.

28)Answer: D.

1 year = 365 days, 1 day = 24 hours

1 year = 365 × 24 = 8,760 hours

29)Answer: B.

Each game 45 minutes, therefore 3 games took 3*45 =135 minutes. 25 minutes between each game. There are 30 minutes in total between 3 games. (between game 1 and 2, 15 minutes and between game 2 and 3, 15 minutes)

Leon arrives 25 minutes before first game and left 15 minutes after the last game.

In total, he was 135 +30 + 25 + 15 = 205 minutes at the soccer field.

30)Answer: C.

To round numbers to the nearest ten thousand, make the numbers whose last four digits are 0001 through 4999 into the next lower number that ends in 0000. For example, 54,424 rounded to the nearest ten thousand would be 50,000. Choice C is correct because last four digits of 56,824,720 is less than 4,999.

Practice Test 2

SBAC - Mathematics

Answers and Explanations

1) Answer: A.

Use area of rectangle formula.

Area = length × width

The length of the rectangle is about 4 inches and its width is about 3 inches. Therefore, the area of the rectangle is 4 × 3 = 12 inches.

2) Answer: C.

7 days = 1 week

42 days = (42 ÷ 7) 6 weeks

3) Answer: C.

The football team should buy 12 uniforms and each uniform cost $35. Therefore, they should pay (12× $ 35) $420.

Choice C is correct answer:

$(35 \times 10) + (35 \times 2) = 350 + 70 = \$420$

4) Answer: C.

18 + Z = 9886. Therefore, Z = 86 − 18 = 68

Let's review the options provided.

A. 86 − 18 = Z   Yes! This is true. 86 − 18 = 68

B. 86 − Z = 18   Yes! This is true. 86 − 68 = 18

C. Z − 18 = 86   No! This is not true. 68 − 18 = 50

D. Z + 18 = 86   Yes! This is true. 68 + 18 = 86

Option C is the only option that is NOT true.

5) Answer: B.

Three – digit odd numbers that have a 7 in the hundreds place and a 5 in the tens place are 751, 753, 755, 777, 759.

Option B, 757, is the answer.

6) Answer: D.

$70 \times 42 = 2,940$

7) Answer: B.

Tam wants to divide his 360 cards into boxes of 40 cards.

Therefore, he needs $360 \div 40 = 9$ boxes.

8) Answer: C.

The clock shows 2:15 in the morning. 4 hours ago, it was 10:15 PM.

30 minutes before that was 9:45 PM.

9) Answer: D

We round the number up to the nearest ten if the last digit in the number is 5, 6, 7, 8, or 9.

We round the number down to the nearest ten if the last digit in the number is 1, 2, 3, or 4.

If the last digit is 0, then we do not have to do any rounding, because it is already to the ten.

Therefore, rounded number of 755 to the nearest ten is 760.

10) Answer: C.

The number of votes for Football was 10, for basketball was 5, for soccer was 7, and for volleyball was 3. Only table C shows all these numbers correctly.

11) Answer: D.

There are 100 equal parts. 89 parts are shaded. It's equal to $\frac{89}{100}$ or

0.89

12) Answer: B.

Choice C shows the numbers in order from least to greatest.

$23,086 < 26,307 < 28,751 < 29,980$

13) Answer: B.

$6.0 - 4.15 = 1.85$

14) Answer: B.

Add adult tickets and children's ticket that have been sold.

$$\frac{46}{100} + \frac{3}{10} = \frac{46}{100} + \frac{30}{100} = \frac{46+30}{100} = \frac{76}{100} = \frac{19}{25}$$

15) Answer: A.

This angle is less than 90°. Only choice A shows angle less than 90°.

16) Answer: A.

$\frac{15}{100}$ is equal to 0.15

17) Answer: D.

Only on option D, all shapes have at least one set of parallel side

and one set of perpendicular side.

18) Answer: A.

Add the number of students at the library and number of students

in classroom.

$75 + 52 = 127$

19) Answer: C.

For the height of 1 centimeter we have 5 pennies, therefore, for

the height of 7 centimeters, we have 5 × 7 pennies.

20) Answer: D.

The first model from left is divided into 6 equal parts. 3 out of 6 parts are shaded. The fraction for this model is $\frac{3}{6} = \frac{1}{2}$. The second model is divided into 8 equal parts. 3 out of 8 parts are shaded. Therefore, the fraction of the shaded parts for this model is $\frac{3}{8}$.

These two models represent different fractions.

21) Answer: B.

$81 \div A = 9$, therefore,

$A = 81 \div 9$

$A = 9$

22) Answer: A.

When rounding to the nearest thousand, you will need to look at the last three digits. If the last three digits is less than 499, rounds down the number ending with three zeros.

On the other hand, if the last three digits is 500 or more, round up the next ending with three zeros. Since, in the number 5,338, the number 338 is smaller than 499, then round the number to 5,000.

23) Answer: B.

$\frac{325}{1000}$ is equal to 0.325

24) Answer: B.

15 ÷ 5 = 3

25) Answer: C.

$\frac{8}{10}$ is equal to 0.8

26) Answer: C.

Only option C fits Emma's description.

27) Answer: C.

17 × 23 = 391

28) Answer: C.

$$\frac{8}{10} - \frac{7}{10} = \frac{1}{10}$$

29) Answer: A.

If one box has 100 flashcards, therefore, 66 boxes have the capacity of (66 × 100) 6,600 flashcards.

30) Answer: C.

0.76 is equal to $\frac{76}{100}$.

"End"

Made in the USA
Las Vegas, NV
13 January 2025